THE WINGS
OF GOD

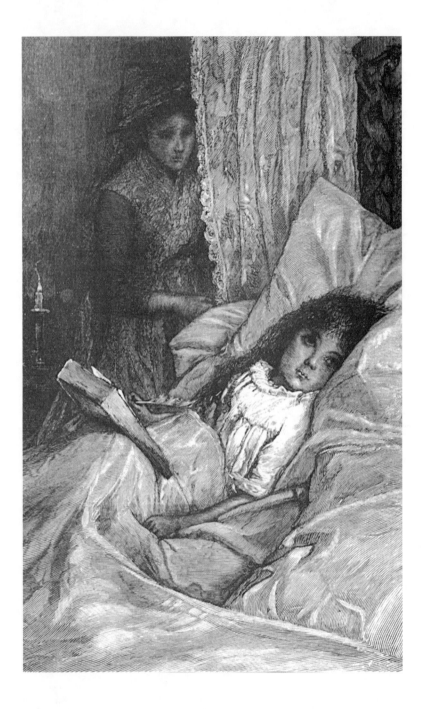

Joe Wheeler

THE WINGS
OF GOD

Miraculous Stories

of Our Lord and

His Angels at Work

WATERBROOK
PRESS

THE WINGS OF GOD
PUBLISHED BY WATERBROOK PRESS
2375 Telstar Drive, Suite 160
Colorado Springs, Colorado 80920
A division of Random House, Inc.

All scripture quotations, unless otherwise indicated, are taken from the *King James Version* of the Bible. Scripture quotations marked (NLT) are taken from the *Holy Bible,* New Living Translation, copyright © 1996. Used by permission of Tyndale House Publishers, Inc., Wheaton, Illinois 60189. All rights reserved.

Woodcut illustrations are from the library of Joe Wheeler.

ISBN 1-57856-320-8

Published in association with the literary agency of Alive Communications, Inc., 7680 Goddard Street, Suite 200, Colorado Springs, CO 80920.

Library of Congress Cataloging-in-Publication Data
The wings of God : miraculous stories of Our Lord and his angels at work / [compiled by] Joe Wheeler.—1st ed.
     p.   cm.
  ISBN 1-57856-320-8
  1. Miracles.   2. Angels.   I. Wheeler, Joe L., 1936–
BT97.2.W487 2000
231.7'3—dc21

                                                            00-043248

Printed in the United States of America
2000—First Edition

10 9 8 7 6 5 4 3 2 1

Blessed indeed am I to have a great-aunt who opens the door into my own past for me. She is remarkable in that not only does she clearly remember the early days of close to a century ago, but she also has not lost a beat in terms of the zeitgeist of today. What a joy to open the collection with her memorable story, "He Shall Give His Angels Charge over You."

Arna Bontemps (one of America's greatest poets) told me not long before he died, at a public reading he did at Vanderbilt University, that Vernon Berry (my late great-uncle) was, at Pacific Union College, the only student he considered to be a greater writer than he. Uncle Vernon went on to become a poet himself, but never of the international stature of Bontemps.

So it gives me great pleasure to dedicate this book of Providence stories to this couple who dedicated their lives to God in mission service.

Table of Contents

He that dwelleth in the secret place of the most High shall abide
under the shadow of the Almighty.
I will say of the LORD, He is my refuge and my fortress: my God;
in him will I trust.
Surely he shall deliver thee from the snare of the fowler, and from
the noisome pestilence.
He shall cover thee with his feathers and under his wings shalt
thou trust: his truth shall be thy shield and buckler.
Thou shalt not be afraid for the terror by night...nor for the
destruction that wasteth at noonday.
A thousand shall fall at thy side, and ten thousand at thy right hand;
but it shall not come nigh thee.
Only with thine eyes shalt thou behold and see the reward of the
wicked.
Because thou hast made the LORD, which is my refuge, even the
most High, thy habitation;
There shall no evil befall thee, neither shall any plague come
nigh thy dwelling.
For he shall give his angels charge over thee, to keep thee in all
thy ways.
They shall bear thee up in their hands, lest thou dash thy foot
against a stone.
Thou shalt tread upon the lion and adder: the young lion and the
dragon shalt thou trample under feet.
Because he hath set his love upon me, therefore will I deliver him:
I will set him on high, because he hath known my name.
He shall call upon me, and I will answer him: I will be with him
in trouble; I will deliver him, and honour him.
With long life will I satisfy him, and shew him my salvation.

PSALM 91

In the Shadow
of His Wings

Trouble. When Christian men, women, and children, down through the ages, have been in trouble—life-threatening trouble—chances are they turned first to David's ninety-first Psalm in their search for answers, for hope itself. Its words, phrases, and lines have such potential to engrave themselves in the individual and collective hearts of mankind that it is virtually impossible to overemphasize this scripture's impact.

Or the beauty of each generation's rediscovery of it.

Thus the thought came to us: *Wouldn't it be special to assemble a collection of stories that spoke to the words of Psalm 91?* What a source of encouragement and joy such a collection might be! This book is our answer to that question.

It is said that there are no atheists in foxholes. If that be true, then there must be something about life-threatening trouble that brings even wanderers back to God. It is easy to be self-sufficient when everything is going right, but when we see that our next breath may very well be our last; when the person we love most is crippled, incapacitated, or dying; all life's priorities suddenly rearrange themselves. Our mortality (or death) smashes our smug answers into smithereens (a Gaelic word meaning "blown to bits").

Psalm 91, having apparently been penned by the Shepherd King thousands of years ago, was written using metaphoric imagery common at that time, a time when in war, death came from such weapons as swords, spears, javelins, and arrows; shields or fortresses provided one's only protection. The first thirteen verses are written from the vantage point of David, a man who knew intimately the fear of being pursued by enemies. Verse fourteen marks a dramatic shift, when God Himself dramatically steps in and ratifies the Psalm's promises.

The first part of the psalm testifies to the close communion the psalmist has with the Almighty. That it is reciprocal is shown by the writer's ability to find protection in the fortress that is God. "In God we trust" is found on the very coins we use in everyday life and evidently is based on the second verse of this psalm. The Hebrew word used for shield (*sinnah*) in verse four refers to the type of shield that protects not just part of the body, but all of it.

Beginning in verse three the psalmist gets specific: Using a bird-like metaphor, he states that God will deliver us from the snares hunters set out in order to catch and kill. The noisome pestilence could be interpreted as a plague of destruction. In any case, the psalmist finds ultimate sanctuary under God's wings, where he is covered by His feathers. No matter whether the enemy come owl-like at night or as a deadly arrow by day, the psalmist is confident in the protection extended not only to him, but to each of us as well. Even though tens of thousands fall all around us, our God will watch over us. David's confidence is bolstered by the promise of guardian angelship: They will lift us up lest we stumble and will protect us from lions, serpents, and dragons (probably sea leviathans).

Then God steps in with an amazing promise for those who love Him. We need not rely merely on David's conviction; we have a promise direct from the Almighty to personally protect us, answer us, deliver us from trouble, honor us, and provide us with salvation.

How God Fulfills This Promise

The stories in this collection reveal that God finds a multitude of ways to respond to our prayers and needs. In some cases the response either borders on the miraculous or simply *is*. In other cases, both the prayer request and the answer are about needs so apparently insignificant that we wonder why God would take the time to meet them. In some cases people fail to offer a prayer at all, yet God responds to their needs anyway. In still other cases God requires the heart of the praying person to be changed or softened until it meets the conditions of "setting our love upon Him," such as divesting the request of selfish conditions or demands.

Some of these stories bring God directly into narrative. Sometimes He is a presence, sometimes a voice, sometimes part of a dream, sometimes a feeling or impression. In some stories God Himself, as God the Son, seems to step into the river of a person's life. Similar variables are also found in the stories involving angels. Some of the stories incorporate angels in human form who step in to rescue, warn, encourage, or comfort. Some of the accounts don't feature divine or angelic creatures at all; nevertheless, they do reveal God's providence at work in our lives. God might use the elements, for example (hurricanes, blizzards, fog, darkness, drought, fire, flood, and so on), to accomplish His will.

Perhaps most special and surprising of all, story after story reveals that God measures the significance of things with a different perspective than we do. He takes time out of His incredibly hectic schedule to respond to even the most simple requests: to ride a Shetland pony, to get a fire started in a frigid room, to make a success of a business, to find the right kind of employee, to get to a speaking appointment on time, to buy a piece of land for a reasonable price, to have water for a children's summer camp, to find a vacuum bag at half price—all these stories and others bring home the conviction that nothing is too small or insignificant for the Lord. The God who notices the fall of a sparrow, who even counts the hairs on our heads, is a God even a child—or perhaps *especially* a child—could not help but love!

WINGS

What is it about wings that fascinates us so? Perhaps because for thousands of years we were earthbound. We could move, at fastest, at the speed of a galloping horse. Oh, we could dream that we had the wings of Icarus and Daedalus, that we might soar at will like the birds we see everywhere. Today's technology has made it possible for each of us to borrow wings, which enable us to travel so fast that we can get to places (thanks to the vagaries of time zones) before we began; we can even soar into outer space. Tragically, those wings can also malfunction, and all those dependent on them hurtle earthward to their deaths.

The Bible is full of references to wings, most often associated with God's messengers, the angels. Because of these miraculously powerful wings, in our worst troubles we dream of what scholars call *deus ex machina:* When all human options fail, a supernatural power sweeps down out of the sky to save us.

Interestingly enough, Psalm 91 makes use of two wing metaphors. First is the powerful eagle-like image, a winged entity capable of bearing us up out of harm's way à la *deus ex machina*; second is a chicken-like image ("He shall cover thee with his feathers, and under his wings shalt thou trust"), reminding us of Christ's words recalled by Luke, the physician: "Oh Jerusalem, Jerusalem…how often would I have gathered thy children together, as a hen doth gather her brood under her wings, and ye would not" (Luke 13:34).

Given the prevalence of wing imagery in Scripture, I have been amazed to discover that in contemporary society's documented angel appearances, almost invariably the heavenly beings appear sans wings and robe, instead blending in with the fashion norms of the time. (Only now, in the space age, are we belatedly realizing that wings, instead of speeding flight, may actually inhibit or slow it.) Obviously, this makes it harder to differentiate between the humans God uses in His service and the celestial beings in such accounts—hence the large number of stories that use the absence of footprints or tracks as authentication of an angel's appearance.

Let's face it: Providence stories can sometimes be a bit disturbing, especially when the elements of coincidence and chance are stirred in. For instance, when one of us has a close call on the highway, an observer may say, "Your guardian angel must have been working overtime," whether we know this is true or not. I have read anthologies of Angel stories—most often unauthenticated—which more appropriately should have carried the title, *Stories of Coincidence and Luck.* It is because of this presence of both kinds of stories that I continually seek divine guidance in putting a collection like this together.

Intriguing to me as well are the characteristics of angels in contemporary stories. They tend to be spare of speech (speaking rarely, and only when they absolutely *have* to) and well-dressed (never flamboyant or directing attention to themselves, however). Most are adult-looking, tending to be males ranging in appearance from young adults to senior citizens. They tend to avoid direct eye contact, but their eyes are piercing when it does occur. Invariably they are kind and empathetic of human suffering and stress, especially where children are concerned, and are almost always helpful, not shirking even the most menial of household tasks. They are as likely to respond to simple, bread-and-butter requests as to those that have to do with life or death implorings. In life or death situations, they are likely to physically remove a threatened person from harm's way if seconds are too few for conversation. When there is a need for the appearance of a large force, especially when attackers are seeking to kill, they often appear in groups and are likely to move aggressively against attackers to put them out of commission in emergency situations. They *never* act contrary to God's laws and directives, which is a quick way to dispose of pseudo-angels scripted by Hollywood! In cases where they are unseen, only a voice, their counsel tends to be extremely concise and usually is delivered in the form of commands, which they repeat up to three times, each with stronger emphasis, the third occurrence being almost impossible to hold out against. They are unlikely to appear unless they are summoned by the individual in trouble or by a godly individual who summons them on behalf of such a person.

A PERSONAL NOTE

I have always believed in angels—believed in them, yes; internalized them, no. I knew the Bible was full of them, and I felt confident that a guardian angel watched over me, but until recently they did not seem three-dimensional to me—not quite real.

One reason they didn't really crystallize in my head was that no one mental picture would stay in focus. Ezekiel and John the Revelator's angels seemed so grand, so terror-inducing, so awe-inspiring, that they remained completely outside the pale of my understanding. I could conceptualize a little better the other biblical angels, but never could I seriously envision them without wings or ancient-world attire. Then there were the scriptural stories that depict God (in most cases, God the Son) in an angelic role. These made me wonder how many Angel stories were really God stories, resulting in further blurring of the angel image in my mind. Complicating the matter even more is the angel/God mythology depicted by the celluloid media, the best-known being Clarence, of Frank Capra's 1946 creation *It's a Wonderful Life,* who happened to be in search of wings. (I do not even stir in the most recent anthropomorphic media depictions: angels saddled with all the sinful drives of the human species. These trouble me greatly because they are so blatantly nonbiblical—unless, of course, they are attempting to depict those who long ago cast their lot with Lucifer.)

As I discovered the stories now contained in this collection, I began to gain, ever so gradually, like seeing a negative developing in a darkroom tray, a new perspective on God, a perspective I never had before.

My own story at the end of the collection reflects a perspective reinforced by all the stories that precede it: that of God as a Grand Chessmaster or Master Choreographer (affirmed scripturally by Psalm 139). God is clearly not in time as we are, but I suspect He sees all of us in a kind of three-dimensional celestial grid. On that grid, every thought, every word, every act, every interaction, has an effect of some kind, similar to a tightly woven spider web, any part of which cannot be touched without causing its entirety to vibrate. Other than the power of choice God has given to each of us, a wild card His omniscience is forced to take into consideration, God must have very few surprises. It is crystal clear to me that God is also somewhat like an air-traffic controller: At any given millisecond He knows (by His "Global Positioning Powers") where each of us is, where we are going, how fast we are going, our moods, our frustrations, our troubles, our agonies, our joys, our needs. Thus He is able, as you will see in the following stories, to set up anything-but-chance meetings that may change the course of a life or avert tragedy.

CODA

Just as my life has been enriched and changed by these stories, my prayer is that your life will be equally blessed, and that you will, in the process of reading them, gain a fresh concept of God's day-by-day interaction in our lives. I would welcome hearing about this impact and the changes that result, as well as any stories you've come to love.

I look forward to hearing from you—and please keep the stories, responses, and suggestions coming. And not just Angel and Providence stories. I am putting together collections of other genres as well. You may contact me by writing to:

Joe Wheeler, Ph.D.
c/o WaterBrook Press
2375 Telstar Drive, Suite 160
Colorado Springs, CO 80920

One

SURELY HE SHALL DELIVER US

*Blessed be the LORD, who hath not given us as a prey to their
teeth. Our soul is escaped as a bird out of the snare of the
fowlers: the snare is broken, and we are escaped. Our help is
in the name of the LORD, who made heaven and earth.*

PSALM 124:6-8

Over the course of researching stories that recount the miraculous ways in which God intervenes in our lives, I prayed that God would bring to mind incidents in which I and those dearest to me had received angelic protection. Instances that came to mind had to do with preservation from death or incapacity in accidents or near accidents (some of which were such close calls that they truly did border on the miraculous). I suspect, in most cases, we aren't fully aware of God's delivering hand in the events of our lives. Perhaps we chalk up too much to coincidence. Even so, I am confident that the Lord and His angels have intervened time after time in each of our lives, as confident as the Auntie of Muriel Parfitt's story in this section:

> We were surrounded by wolves all right. But our never-
> failing God was watching over us. No matter what we do
> or where we are, God sees us. He always takes care of His

children, and we have positive proof of that fact too, because when Uncle John and our friend looked for something with which to build a fire [to ward off the wolves], they felt the trees around them and found that we were standing by an evergreen tree.

And no ordinary evergreen was this, as Auntie's heavenly Father knew, but the *very* evergreen that was needed, the evergreen to which only He could have so miraculously led the surrounded party.

Not until we get to heaven will we really know how many times these divine interventions saved us from disaster or death. Still, on some occasions, such as those presented here, His role is undeniable.

He Shall Give His Angels Charge over You

LOIS WHEELER BERRY

I grew up on this story, hearing it retold many times during my childhood and adolescence. I don't believe it is mere coincidence that my grandfather's sister—very much alive, memory razor-sharp, and in her nineties, who heard the story over and over, firsthand at her father's knee—agreed to write it out for me by hand, and then faxed it to me. I also referred to another account written by one of my cousins (Dorothy Johnson Muir's "Faith," published in the August 2, 1938, Youth's Instructor). Essentially, what follows is Lois Berry's story, with Dorothy Muir's account and my own memories intertwining on occasion.

If ever a man had absolute faith in his God, it was my father. And God honored that faith many, many times. But while many miraculous happenings were tied to his medical ministry, there was one story that took place even before medical school—before I was born, in fact (one reason I've always envied my three older siblings). During my growing-up years, no story did we children request more often than this one, and Father never tired of telling it.

During the early 1890s, Father, for a time, sold Christian

books. This particular story took place during the summer of '92. Father had been taking book orders in the then rather wild Shasta and Modoc Counties of northeastern California. So spectacularly beautiful was the scenery that Father determined to bring Mother along in the fall when he delivered the books.

So it was that, after camp meeting in Stockton, Father hitched his two horses to the wagon (already heavily loaded with books and supplies, for there were then mighty few places to stop for food), signaled Mother and the three children to board the wagon, slapped the reins on the horses' rumps, and set off. Vacations were rare in those days; consequently, the children found this camping trip incredibly exciting.

Father made several book deliveries in the Redding and Mount Shasta area. (Mount Shasta, at 14,161 feet, dominates the skyline of that part of the state. Always there is snow on it, but in those days there was a lot more snow than we see today.) Afterward, the family headed up the steep road toward the eastern side of the Sierra Nevada. The weight of all those books, five people, food, and camping quilts guaranteed a slow trip, but the children didn't care, for that meant more nights camping out under the stars.

Finally, as they approached the highest summit on the route, Father joyfully remembered that there was an inn there—fittingly called Paradise Inn. How wonderful to sleep in a real bed for one night!

Alas! When they arrived about sundown, there were only smoldering ruins, a stark fireplace alone still standing, legacy of a swift-moving forest fire.

Father managed to find a place to camp under a few trees that had somehow survived the fire. Mother fixed supper, and everyone else set up camp. After supper, at worship, Father asked the Lord to send His angels to protect them during the night.

The cold at that elevation was bone chilling—winter was in the air. Finally, Father and Mother held a family council: *What should they do?* Father remembered that there was a house about six miles further, on the other side of the mountain. If they kept going, surely they'd be offered hospitality. The children, teeth chattering and unable to get warm, were easy to persuade. So they loaded all the bedding back into the wagon, rounded up the weary horses, and rehitched them to the wagon. Before slapping the reins, Father once again prayed that the Lord's angels would protect them during the long descent.

Night fell quickly. The darkness was so thick they could almost feel it. Not being able to see the road, Father loosened the reins, tied them to the whipstock, and left it up to the horses to find their way down. It was at this part of the story that Father's voice always slowed as he struggled for emotional control. You see, horse-drawn wagon travel was incredibly noisy; the horses' every move, every step, every snort, every shake of the reins, could be clearly heard. Same with the wagon; the great solid rims were never quiet as they battled through dirt, gravel, and rocks; the wind whipped at the canvas, and the wooden chassis with its leather supports continually creaked and groaned. It was for this reason that none of the five ever forgot that night. Not only could they not see in the pitch-blackness—*they could not hear!* The wagon did not squeak; the wheels could not be heard as they turned, nor could the horses' hooves—it was eerily silent! The travelers only sensed that they were moving.

Occasionally, they would feel a jolt, and twice the wagon came to a complete stop. In each case, Father slowly got out and groped his way toward the horses' heads, then stooped down to detect the problem. In each case, he encountered logs, logs he was able—somehow—to move. Then he groped his way back to the horses, then back to the wagon, reboarded it, and signaled the horses that the way was clear. Once again there was absolute silence.

Not long after the second stop, everyone experienced a hard jolt. Immediately, the jogging of the horses could be heard again, the wagon wheels could be heard again, and all the multitudinous wagon squeaks could be heard again.

After what seemed an entire night (but in reality, only about four hours), they saw, off in the distance—faintly at first—a light in a window. As they drew nearer, dogs began to bark, and then a man came out, with a lantern in his hand, curious as to who these unexpected visitors might be and where they might have come from. Father politely introduced himself and then explained how they had planned to stay at Paradise Inn, but finding only ruins there had just kept going, hoping they could make it down the mountain safely, and trusting they would be welcome to stay overnight at this rancher's house.

The rancher didn't believe him at all, and retorted, "Now, really, no joking, where did you come from?"

Father again reaffirmed his story.

The rancher exploded, "Why, man, you're crazy! No one has made it through in over five days. It is impossible! Just today a man tried to go through on horseback, but he could not!" And thus, preposterous to imagine that a *wagon* could get through! "A terrible forest fire has burned everything—trees, brush, and houses."

But Father stuck to his story. Once again he asked if they could stay overnight, and if there was feed and shelter for the horses. "Of course," answered the rancher. After the children were put to bed, Father went out to unhitch and tend to the horses, only to find out that the kind rancher had already taken care of them. Before retiring, Father and Mother knelt down and offered a prayer of thanksgiving.

The following morning, the rancher again asked Father for the truth. Once again the answer was the same. The rancher then showed Father the road and the terrain over which he would have had to travel. As Father's gaze took in that impassable vista of fallen trees and smoldering logs, he finally understood the rancher's disbelief. So Father explained to him how they had prayed for angelic protection before leaving the pass.

The last thing the family saw as they left the ranch was their host, with a gun on his shoulder, retracing their route of the night before, walking between their wagon wheel tracks toward the spot where the tracks inexplicably disappeared.

Led by Angels

Muriel Parfitt

Ice closed in on them first, then night, and then wolves.
What should they do?

Two pajama-clad little girls ran to get the coveted place at the foot of Auntie's chair. "Tell us a story," they said breathlessly as they seated themselves and wiggled around to get comfortable.

"If you two could stop wiggling and sit still, maybe I would," she laughed.

"Oh, we will," they agreed as they curled up on the rug at her feet.

Auntie settled back in her easy chair, and her eyes had a far-away look as she began her story.

"When I was young my husband and I lived in northern Wisconsin. At that time it was very wild and unsettled territory. Each summer we cut our wood for the winter at a particular camp. Our camp was some distance from any settlement, and the shortest way to civilization was to travel by canoe through the lakes. The lake on which we had our camp led to other lakes, and by following these we could make our way back to the settlement in which we lived.

"It was getting late in the fall and the nights were becoming colder. We would find ice on some of the puddles in the morning, and often the days were bleak and cheerless.

"Uncle John and a friend, who also had been getting wood, came in one day blowing on their fingers to warm them and said that they thought we had better start back to civilization as soon as possible. We finished our work at camp and made preparations to leave. Finally all was in readiness, so I took a sandwich for each of us and helped the men pack and load our light canoe. With good traveling we would be back in the settlement by suppertime. We ate dinner early, closed camp, and set out for home.

"The canoe drifted along with the current, and I settled back to enjoy the scenery. The clear blue of the sky was mirrored in the deep blue of the lake. Now and then fleecy clouds drifted by, and I watched as they passed over the sun and made shadows in the valleys and sunshine on the hills. Squirrels chattered noisily at each other as they gathered nuts and chased each other through the trees along the shore. Occasionally a deer appeared, and the jays would set the forest ringing with their cries of 'Thief, thief.' We laughed and talked as we paddled along, the cold air adding to our appetites, and we thought of the pleasant, warm supper we would have back at the settlement.

"The sun was beginning to lower and the air was getting colder as we entered the next lake. A thin crust of ice confronted us. A look of anxiety passed over the men's faces as they started through the lake adjoining that one. The ice was thicker and they could hardly paddle. The ice rubbed our canoe much harder and pressed against our frail craft. The men held a consultation. If we kept on, the ice might possibly wear a hole in our thin canoe, or it might freeze the canoe solid, so that we could not move. A trip along the shore would take us much longer and would mean a long walk around the lake.

"We knew of an old man who lived in a cabin on the lake, so we decided to land our canoe. Our friend took a packsack and the case containing his gun, Uncle John took what he could carry, and I brought our little rifle. We left our canoe at the portage and started for the cabin.

"The forest was darker than it had been on the lake, but we hurried along as best we could. All went well for a time, but it soon was so dark that we could barely see where we were going. Suddenly we heard a lone, wavering howl ahead on the trail. It sounded through the forest and was answered by howls on all sides of us. I shivered, and it was not from the cold this time. Fear made me feel cold and clammy. The howls of the wolves grew closer, and the men stopped and threw down their packs. By this time it was so dark we could not see anything."

The little girls were sitting up now, their eyes bright with excitement.

"You mean you were surrounded by wolves? Were they big? What happened? What did you do?" they asked, running their sentences together as well as their words.

Auntie smiled. "We were surrounded by wolves all right. But our never-failing God was watching over us. No matter what we do or where we are, God sees us. He always takes care of His children, and we have positive proof of that fact too, because when Uncle John and our friend looked for something with which to build a fire, they felt the trees around them and found that we were standing by an evergreen tree. Now you know, wild animals are afraid of fire, and with the boughs of an evergreen tree to throw on a fire to make it flare up, we knew we were safe.

"The men worked feverishly to start the fire by picking up some dry leaves and pulling off some branches of the evergreen. They looked through all their pockets for matches but could not find any. Our friend remembered that I had some in my apron pocket, so he told me to get them for him quickly. But I was too frightened to move. He ran over to me, took the matches out of my pocket, and started the fire before I could do anything.

"Uncle John and I kept putting things on the fire to burn while our friend took his gun from his case and began to assemble it. How he got it together in the flickering of the firelight is more proof than ever that Jesus does help.

"The wolves were closing in, and their howls were so loud that we could not even talk to each other except by shouting. Even then we sometimes could not hear each other.

"After about two hours of continual howling the wolves grew silent. But we knew they were there, for we could hear the twigs snapping under the weight of their heavy bodies as they walked around us. Our friend wanted to shoot into the darkness where he heard the wolves, but after discussing it with us he decided against taking this action. In case the wolves should still make an attack on us, the few shells he had would be needed, so we could not spare even one.

"All that night the wolves were there, and all that night we felt as though someone were there with us, protecting us. We accepted the verse 'The angel of the Lord encampeth round about them' as though it had been written especially for us.

"Just as the sun started streaking the sky with rays of light, the wolves gave what sounded to me like disgusted grunts and disappeared into the shadows.

"We waited until the sun had risen and daylight was well upon us before we moved. We looked around us, and in the light of day saw something that will ever convince us that Jesus does see and hear us when we call on Him. Girls, we were standing by the only evergreen tree that was around there. All the other trees, if they would burn, would not have given as great a light as the evergreen. Do you think it was just luck that made us stop in that certain place? No, girls, you can be sure God had seen our need and led us to that spot. We thanked Him again and again for His watchcare over us."

The Clock That Struck Thirteen

W. A. SPICER

*An unforgettable account of God's incredible choreography
was told by the Rev. J. Bounsall, of Ottery, St. Mary,
in Devon, England, over 150 years ago.*

"It was about the midnight hour in the town of Plymouth, many years ago," he said, "when two men stood close to the great clock of the town and heard it strike the hour. Both men remarked to each other that it had struck thirteen times instead of twelve. One of these men was a gentleman by the name of Captain Jarvis.

"Not very long afterward, this same Captain Jarvis awoke very early one morning, got up, dressed, and went down to the front door of his house. When he opened it, he was surprised to find his groom standing there, with his horse saddled and bridled, ready for him to mount.

"'I had a feeling that you would be wanting your horse, sir,' he said, 'so I could not stay longer in my bed, and just got it ready for you!'

"The captain was astonished at first, and then mounted the horse and rode off. He did not direct his steed where to go, but just let him go wherever he chose. Down to the riverside they went, close to the spot where the ferryboat took passengers across. What, then, was the captain's amazement when he saw the ferryman there, waiting with his boat to ferry him across at that early hour!

"'How are you here so early, my man?' he inquired at once.

"'I couldn't rest in my bed, sir, for I had a feeling I was wanted to ferry someone across.'

"The captain and horse both got into the boat, and were safely conveyed to the other side.

"Again Captain Jarvis gave his horse his own way as to where he should go. On and on they went, until at length they came to a large country town.

"The captain asked a passerby if there was anything of interest going on in the town.

"'No, sir; nothing but the trial of a man for murder.'

"The captain rode to the place where the trial was going on, dismounted, and entered the building. As he walked in, he heard the judge say, addressing the prisoner, 'Have you anything to say for yourself—anything at all?'

"'I have nothing to say, sir, except that I am an innocent man, and that there is only one man in all the world who could prove my innocence, but I do not know his name nor where he lives. Some weeks ago we stood together in the town of Plymouth when it was midnight, and we both heard the great town clock strike thirteen instead of twelve, and remarked it to each other. If he were here, he could speak for me, but my case is hopeless, as I cannot get him.'

"'I am here! I am here!' shouted the captain, from behind. 'I was the man who stood at night beside the great Plymouth clock, and heard it strike thirteen, instead of twelve. What the prisoner says is absolutely true; I identify him as the man. On the night of

the murder, at the very time it was committed, that man was with me, at Plymouth, and we remarked to each other how remarkable it was that the clock should strike thirteen at the midnight hour.'

"The condemned man was thus proved innocent, and was at once set free."

Broken Chains, Open Doors

EDITED BY W. A. SPICER

Not just in Bible times have prisons been miraculously opened.

It was a godly band of believers who were guided by God's providence out of the house of bondage in Moravia to the estates of Count Zinzendorf, in Saxony, there to form the vanguard of the modern missionary army. It was on these estates that they founded their town of Herrnhut. In the escape from Moravia, some of them bore witness to deliverances that they could ascribe only to the direct intervention of the angels of the Lord.

David Nitschmann was one of their leaders. In his own story of his life he speaks of "the miraculous escape," which the Lord vouchsafed to him in Moravia. He and a number of the brethren were arrested and put in irons in the prison. Nitschmann tells how he and another were especially impressed one night that they should escape, and how the way was opened:

> One Thursday evening I told my brethren that I had
> thoughts of leaving them that night. "And I too," instantly

added David Schneider; "I mean to go with you." We had to wait till eleven. Not knowing how I should be able to get rid of my irons, I laid hands upon the padlock which fastened them, to try to open it with a knife; and behold it was opened!

I began to weep for joy, and I said to Schneider, "Now I see it is the will of God that we should go."

We removed the irons from our feet, we took leave of the other brethren in profound silence, and crossed the court to see if we could find a ladder. I went as far as the principal passage, which was secured by two doors; and I found the first opened, and the second also. This was a second sign to us that we were to go. Being once out of the castle, we hung our irons on the wall, and we crossed the garden to reach my dwelling, where we waited awhile, that I might tell my wife how she should proceed when I sent some one to fetch her."
— *"Suppressed Evidence" by Thomas Boys*

They got away and ultimately reached Herrnhut in safety. The authorities ordered their wives to send someone after them as they fled to bring them back. Compelled to act, a friend, David Hinkel, went after them. After some days he returned, unable to overtake the two brethren. Bost tells the sequel in his *History of the Bohemian and Moravian Brethren:*

The judge ordered [Hinkel] to be immediately committed to prison, and told him he should be hanged for aiding the escape of his brethren. "That," he said coolly, "is as God wills it; if He does not purpose it, it will not be."

They thrust him into a cold, dark hole, where he remained three days without anything to eat or drink.

He was then brought before the judge, half dead with cold, to tell what he knew of the two men who had escaped. As he persisted in declaring that he knew nothing of them, they put him in a warmer place, where they gave him a piece of coarse bread and some dirty water, charging the jailer to watch him carefully. [This charge, it is suggested, reminded Hinkel of the charge to the Philippian jailer, before Paul's deliverance. See Acts 16:23.]…

This appeared to him, he tells us, like an intimation from God to make his escape. He opened the door softly, saw the sentinels placed in such a way that he could pass them without being perceived, by the back gate into the garden, and thence into the village. He walked out in broad day, took leave of some of his brethren, set off in haste for Saxony, and arrived safely at Herrnhut.

No wonder these loyal believers, in the hands of bitter enemies of the truth of God, rejoiced in the ministry of the angels of God, the same who opened prison doors in olden times and struck chains from the hands of the Lord's servants. Bost tells of yet another similar deliverance:

Andrew Beyer was shut up in prison at Kunewalde for more than a year, and tortured, because he would not give up his faith or his connection with the Brethren; but his persecutors could not prevail. They therefore commanded him to be loaded with irons, and cast into a dark and damp dungeon.

The day on which his sentence was to have been executed, David Fritsch, who was in the same prison, happened to push against the door, and the great chain, which was stretched across the outside, gave way. They opened the door, and seeing no sentinels, went home, took their wives and children, one of them only six months old, and fled. After many perils and privations they also arrived safely at Herrnhut.

The covering, protecting hand of the Lord was a very real thing to the faith of these men of God. In dependence upon Him, and seeking His guidance in everything, the exiles built up the settlement at Herrnhut, where they had found refuge, making it a veritable missionary training center. The pious and practical Count Zinzendorf welcomed them as men after his own heart, and by laboring together in the Lord they developed the wonderful Moravian missionary movement, which planted the standard of the gospel in many dark lands over the seas.

Any Deadly Thing

MARJORIE LEWIS LLOYD

It is one thing to say "the Bible is inspired."
It is quite another thing to challenge the laws of chemistry
and risk sudden death on words found in Scripture.

Just such a life-or-death story took place
during the Iron Curtain years in Eastern Europe.

A Christian worker, according to this account, had been arrested and imprisoned. One day he was taken from his cell and led into an interrogation room, where a police officer and a doctor were sitting at a table. Lying open on the table was a Bible, and the prisoner was asked if he believed the book to be the Word of God. He answered that he did. Then he was asked to read Mark 16:18. And he read aloud, "And if they drink any deadly thing, it shall not hurt them."

"Do you believe this part of the Bible too?" the officer demanded. The Christian replied, "Yes."

The officer placed a filled glass on the table and said, "In this glass there is a strong poison. If the book is true, as you insist, it won't hurt you. But to show you we don't play with you, watch this!"

A large dog was brought in and given some of the liquid. In a very few moments the dog was dead.

"Do you still claim that this book you call 'God's Word' is true?"

"Yes, it is God's Word. It is true."

Then, with the doctor looking on, the officer shouted, "Drink the entire glass!"

The Christian asked permission to pray first. He knelt down by the table, took the glass in his hands, and prayed for his family that their faith might not fail. Then he prayed for the officer and the doctor that they, too, might become followers of Christ. Then he said, "Lord, You see how they have challenged You. I am ready to die. But I believe Your Word that nothing will happen to me. Should Your plan be different, I am ready to meet You. My life is in Your hands. May Your will be done."

Then he lifted the glass and drank it down. The doctor and the officer were amazed and not a little surprised. They hadn't expected this. They thought he would break first. Now they watched for him to collapse. He didn't. There was complete silence. The minutes seemed like hours. Finally the doctor felt the prisoner's pulse. It was normal. He continued his examination but could find no symptoms, no evidence of harm. He couldn't hide his astonishment. At last he slumped into his chair, paused a moment, then took his party card from his pocket, tore it in half, and threw it on the floor!

He reached out for the Bible, took it in his hand, and held it reverently. "From today," he said with conviction, "I, too, will believe in this Book. It must be true. I, too, am ready to believe this Christ who did this thing before my eyes!"

How Stanley Met Livingstone

W. A. SPICER

Dr. Livingstone, without provisions, was staring death in the face.
What should he do—what could he do?

❧

It was surely at the hour timed by Providence that Stanley met Livingstone, at Ujiji, in 1871. Rumors had come out of Africa that the missionary explorer was dead. No confirmation of the news could be had, however, and James Gordon Bennett, of the New York *Herald,* joined by the London *Daily Telegraph,* sent Stanley into the unknown interior of Africa with orders to find Livingstone.

Meanwhile, Livingstone had been halted in his quest for information concerning the river systems beyond Tanganyika. The Arabs, with whom he traveled in the Manyuema country, had been so merciless in their treatment of the village people that the missionary could see no way but to leave them and turn back to his base at Ujiji. Notes from Livingstone's journal show how providentially his return fitted into the progress of Stanley's search for him. The inclusion of a few "notes by the way" adds features of interest, though of primary note is the story of Stanley's providential arrival at the very place and time where Livingstone had to have help:

July 14. "I am distressed and perplexed what to do so as not to be foiled, but all seems against me."

July 20. Livingstone leaves for Ujiji.

August 8. A native hidden close by the path throws a spear at him. "As they are expert with the spear, I do not know how it missed, except that he was too sure of his aim, and the good hand of God was upon me.... Another spear was thrown." This also just missed. Then a huge tree fell across the path. Livingstone heard the crack as it started falling, and jumped from under the falling trunk. The lower limbs had rattled off, and he was near the foot of the tree, so that he again escaped. "Three times in one day I was delivered from impending death. My attendants, who were scattered in all directions, came running back to me, calling out, 'Peace! peace! You will finish all your work in spite of these people, and in spite of everything.' Like them, I took it as an omen of good success to crown me yet, thanks to the 'Almighty Preserver of me.'"

September 22. "In the latter part of [the journey back], I felt as if I were dying on my feet."

October 3. "I read the whole Bible through four times while I was in Manyuema."

October 23. Livingstone arrives at Ujiji, his base on the northeastern shore of Lake Tanganyika, expecting to find stores and goods for barter, which he had left in the care of a friendly Arab. Hope of securing comforts and necessaries from this store buoyed up his spirits on the last weary weeks of his march. Upon arriving, however, he found that his rascally friend had stolen and used or sold off all the stores. Livingstone had arrived a mere "ruckle of bones," and now he was stranded indeed. He could only say in his extremity: "I commit myself to the Almighty Disposer of events." But his deliverance was on the way, to arrive in time.

October 24. "I felt in my destitution as if I were the man who went down from Jerusalem to Jericho, and fell among thieves; but I could not hope for priest, Levite, or good Samaritan to come by on either side.... But when my spirits were at their lowest ebb, the good Samaritan was close at hand, for one morning Susi came running, at the top of his speed, and gasped out, 'An Englishman! I see him!' and off he darted to meet him. The American flag at the head of the caravan told me of the nationality of the stranger."

The Delayed Trial

MARJORIE LEWIS LLOYD

Circumstantial evidence. It can hang you out to dry.
How can you prove you didn't really mean
to commit a crime, that it was accidental?

This is the story of a man named Jim, who, without realizing it, carried a pocket calculator he had been looking at out of a store, along with his purchases. When he got to the car, he tossed his packages onto the front seat, and one of them slid to the floor. As he bent over to pick it up, he saw the calculator underneath it. To anyone looking on, of course, it would appear that he was trying to hide it.

Someone *was* looking on. Just at that moment the store owner opened the car door and demanded that Jim get out. He was arrested for shoplifting.

The accusation dealt Jim a serious blow. He and his family were new in the city. Nobody knew him. His job and his reputation were at stake. It was the next day before he could get up courage to tell his wife, Janine, what had happened. "It was so stupid," he said, "so stupid!" He felt he had to plead guilty. After all, the calculator was in his possession when he was arrested. No one would be concerned about whether he *meant* to take it.

He was called before the judge the following Friday to face the charges. The court went through the usual formalities. But when the judge asked if he had anything to say, Jim explained what had happened. The judge interrupted. "Just a minute—are you trying to say that you did not *intend* to take this calculator?"

"No, I did not, Your Honor."

"Then I can't accept your plea of guilty. This case will have to be held over for trial in a criminal court." The trial was set for November 20.

Jim and Janine prayed constantly those days—they prayed as they never had before.

The trial was on a Thursday. Six witnesses testified against Jim. Then his lawyer called for a recess and told Jim he could get off on a technicality: None of the witnesses could prove that the calculator in Jim's possession was the same calculator that had been in the store. Jim didn't want that.

The judge had to leave to catch a plane. Court was adjourned until the next Tuesday.

Jim and Janine kept praying. Janine fasted one day. All that mattered was that she be right with God. Otherwise, how could He hear her prayers? Afterward, she experienced a calm and a peace she had not known before.

On Tuesday, all the judge had to do was sum up his findings and give his verdict. But he added something unexpected. The judge had a story to tell of what had happened to him on Saturday. Shopping in the Redlands Shopping Center, he made several purchases and looked at a number of other items. As he was getting into his car, he suddenly realized he had accidentally picked up an item and brought it out with him. "If I had been stopped then," he told the lawyers, "I would have been in exactly the same predicament as this man."

And then, "Not guilty. Case dismissed."

An Angel Walked

Lois M. Parker

She was a very old woman with a wizened face. People made fun of her—especially her feet. But once one heard her story...

"Have you seen her feet?" The hushed voice of the nurse dropped even lower. "I'll show you."

Nurses see many tragic things. *This must be most unusual,* I thought, *to affect the girl in white in such a way.* I followed.

A tiny wizened face turned to us from the white pillow. I did not notice the age lines or emaciation at first. Dominant as always were her eyes, alert and interested.

She had never been conspicuous in church. Only by accident had I noticed her earnestness in following the services, the radiance in the little aged face bowing in prayer or nodding an unspoken Amen. Her lips had formed the words of the hymns, and one felt that she joined an angel chorus in her mind, though she made no sound.

Now she could attend church no longer. Her labored steps could not carry her to the services she loved, so when she lay in the hospital, with few visitors, I felt that I must go to see her.

"Sophie, here is a visitor," the nurse cheerfully announced. "She is a nurse too. Do you mind if I show her your feet?"

Brightness bloomed in her face as she stretched a hand to me.

"Oh, my friend! It is so good of you to come. Yes, of course, nurse, show her the old stubs. They are good for nothing now, but to remind me that angels walk with men."

The feet. They were purple and swollen beyond much semblance of humanity. The darkened color served to make more distinct the white scars that marred toes, insteps, ankles. The scars were very old, I could see, and I wondered what ordeal had brought them. It was a relief to have them covered again.

Sophie smiled.

"Put them away. No one would want to look at them long. They're no good now, but many and many the mile they have walked. Thirteen children I raised, and worked in the fields besides, so you see they have done their work. Let them rest."

As I held her shrunken hand, the question must have shown on my face.

"You would like to hear a story, ya?"

The forests of Russia, long ago, were thick and dark. Even in the little village, safely shut in by walls and lighted by candles, one could sometimes hear the wolves. No one risked the narrow forest roads at night, and even in daylight the men never went out less than two at a time. But the villagers were comfortable and safe—if they had shelter, wood, and food.

The people of this village belonged to the land, and each family was required to serve their lord for a certain time, to pay for the privilege of living.

At the castle, a long day's drive from the village home, Sophie looked anxiously out over the snowy fields. After so much time there was still no dark speck coming out of the forest, to grow into her father's team and sled.

She was no longer needed, or even wanted, in the castle. Her term of three months' service had been broken by a trip home to care for a dreadfully ill mother, so she had stayed on at the castle two weeks later than the other village young folks.

It would have been such a merry ride home with them, she thought. Those now at the castle were strangers, and uninterested in her, sometimes even mocking her village ways. She was eager to get home, and her father had promised to come for her.

With sudden decision she whipped her babushka over her head and tied it firmly. Long since she had put on her felt boots and overboots. Now, as a "town" girl giggled and pointed at her rustic clothing, Sophie gathered her small bundle of belongings and started out, her determined little chin set.

At first the road was broken. Wood sleds had been out since the new snow. Her feet were as light as her heart as she thought of home and her family.

Long before the tracks ended, the castle fell out of sight. The fields were fewer and the forests were closing in. Before Sophie lay an unbroken trail, a winding white ribbon between dark walls of green. She hesitated, a little doubtful, then reassured herself aloud.

"Father promised he would come for me this morning. Surely, just around a bend or two, I will hear the bells of his sled."

She stepped briskly into the deep snow. It was light and fluffy, quite fresh, and it was not hard walking, even though it came well above the tops of the felt boots. The sun shone, and once in a while the harsh note of a winter bird assured her that the snow had not covered all life.

She was very strong in spite of her small size, and she delighted in the rhythmic swing of walking. It was an hour or more before the stillness of the woods began to oppress, and she slowed, a doubt stirring about the wisdom of going farther.

Snow had begun to work between the tops of the felt boots and her legs. The boots were old and not as snug as they should have been. There was a wet band around the thick woolen stockings where the snow had melted. She dug out some snow, but could feel the wetness going down inside.

Perhaps I should go back, but they don't need me, and there is hardly space for an extra in the girls' room.

As she stood thinking, a faint sound vibrated through the forest. Not sure at first what it was, she turned to listen. Again the distant sound came, and she knew.

She could not go back. There were wolves behind her—far away, but between her and the castle.

She gasped a little but without wasting a moment went on, every step an emphasis to the prayer she whispered. "Lord of heaven, be with me, help me!"

Walking was no longer fun. Her ears were straining, both for the jingle of bells and for the wolves. Sometimes she found herself running and breathless. Then, fighting panic, she walked again.

For long minutes there was silence except for her own breath and footsteps. Silence—perhaps even a half-hour, until the moaning cry came again, always a little closer.

They aren't hunting in earnest or they would come faster, she thought desperately.

Her feet were all wet now inside the boots, and she was tiring. The sun commenced to slip down the western slope, toward early nightfall. A pain pierced her side. When she slowed, attempting to ease it, the eerie call would again spur her on.

Her feet were so cold. If only she could rest—she was getting so tired. It was an effort to push her feet through the snow, and she could no longer lift them very high. The trail behind her was erratic, for she could not walk steadily.

A low branch draped itself over the road. She would go that far at least, before she stopped. Upon reaching the branch she set another goal, farther on.

Like a refrain, her prayer went on and on. She had no more strength to say it aloud. *Father, help me. I need Thee. Help me. Send an angel to help me. Lord of all, be with me*—over and over, with a little change of words, but always the cry, *Help, Lord!*

Her strength failed until she could barely reach a fallen stub. As she leaned against it, with sobbing breath, faintness almost overwhelmed her.

She felt a hand on her shoulder, and a soft, kind voice spoke in her ear. "You cannot rest now, Sophie. Go on."

Stupid with weariness, she turned, but no one was there. Save hers, there were no tracks in the snow. In bewilderment she pushed away from the stub, and from somewhere came renewed strength.

One step after another, one after another, while her mind forgot to listen for the wolves. Her prayer now was partly a plea and partly, faintly, questioning.

Lord, help me. Oh, Father, was it—who was it? No one was there! Oh, be with me, Lord. I know it must have been!

And a throbbing of her heart would send a surge of warmth to her cold hands and almost to her numbed feet. They were no longer cold, which was a relief, though somewhere in the fog of her brain, a warning note tried to get through.

She was tiring again, forgetting the wolves, forgetting everything but shoving first one foot then another through the snow.

The sun was down. In the growing darkness the upward rise looked familiar. It *was* familiar. She had climbed it many times and rested for a while on the log bench at the top, above the village. If only she could get that far.

It seemed an age before she stumbled into the snow-covered seat and fell upon it. Below, the village lights gleamed out on the whiteness.

It was too far. Sophie's head sank and she felt blackness creeping about her. A hand seized her shoulder and shook her into wakefulness.

"Sophie!" Again the clear, gentle voice was insistent. "You cannot rest yet! Go home!"

Against her will, she was raised to her feet and started down the road. Her rebellious legs could not tell when her feet touched the ground, and she stumbled again and again before finally falling against a door.

All at once, her father's face was above her, filled with consternation, lights about her, voices exclaiming, and arms bearing her into warmth that was almost unendurable.

Sophie put her hand out to me again.

"My father never forgave himself. He had good reason not to come, for my uncle had died and was buried that day. I should not have left the castle at all 'til he came, so it was not his fault."

She smiled a little, remembering.

"It was a year before I could stand on my feet. They were frozen solid, and it is a miracle that I did not lose them both. My father would hold me and rock me, night after night, when I could not sleep for the pain."

"They were pretty good feet after a while. Oh, always they were sore, and hurt when it was cold, but I could use them. Now it is time for them to rest. And someday soon—"

The light in her face was pure glory.

"There were no tracks alongside mine on the snow. Someday soon I will see the angel who walked with me!"

Two

HE SHALL COVER US WITH HIS FEATHERS

Father, if thou be willing, remove this cup from me:
nevertheless not my will, but thine, be done.

LUKE 22:42

One of the biggest surprises to come my way during the gestation of this book had to do with the stories in this section. My prior perception of prayer requests was perhaps closest to "He that asketh not, receiveth not." Now, I believe that to be only partly true. The principle is expressed by Catherine Marshall in her story in this section:

"I said, 'God, I don't know who You are. I don't know anything about You. I don't even know how to pray. Just, Lord, have Your own way with me.'"

Though she did not realize it, Maude Blanford had just prayed one of the most powerful of all prayers—the prayer of relinquishment. By getting her own mind and will out of the way, she had opened the door to the Holy Spirit....

Again and again in these Angel/Providence stories we are brought back to a central character trait of the Godhead: God refuses to violate, or even infringe upon, our freedom of choice. C. S. Lewis often speaks about this rather strange trait of God's: The only all-powerful force in all creation adamantly refuses to step in unless asked to do so by even the weakest of His children. On the other hand, He is not unduly responsive to our demands, turning a rather deaf ear to our self-centered "gimmies." *But*, should we wish to access all of the power and energy at the Trinity's command, all we have to do or say…is to surrender, and pray Christ's prayer of relinquishment in the Garden of Gethsemane. Under the protective, omnipotent covering of His wings, we must first hand over to God, not just part of ourselves—but *all* of ourselves.

The Healing of Maude Blanford

CATHERINE MARSHALL

So intrigued was the famous author that she knew she must visit Maude Blanford in person, and hear the incredible story firsthand.

❦

This is a story of a healing, one of the most remarkable I have ever encountered. And yet—to me—the physical miracle is not the chief thing the experience has to say to us.

Healing through faith remains a mystery to me. I have been part of prayer campaigns where it was gloriously granted, and others where, at least in this world, it was not. As a young wife and mother, I myself was wonderfully healed. At the time of Peter Marshall's first heart attack, he was brought back from the brink of death, yet went on into the next life three years later. And despite an all-out prayer effort, the baby daughter born one summer to my son Peter John and his wife Edith lived on this earth but six weeks.

Why? There are no glib answers. I sense that my own questions about healing are shared by scores of honest seekers. Yet in my experience, as God has closed one door, He always has opened another.

So even as I was parting tenderly with my tiny granddaughter, a new friend from Louisville, Kentucky, came through an open door on another side of this difficult question, by telling me of Maude Blanford's healing from terminal cancer twelve years earlier. In the end, I was intrigued enough to fly to Louisville and get the details from the former patient herself.

The woman across the dining table from me had no trace of gray in her reddish hair, though she was past middle age now, a grand-motherly type, comfortable to be with. "How did your—ah, illness begin?" I asked, feeling foolish even asking the question of some-one obviously in such radiant health.

"My left leg had been hurting me," Mrs. Blanford replied. "I thought it was because I was on my feet so much. Finally, when I couldn't stand it any longer, my husband and I decided that I should go to the doctor."

When her family doctor examined her, his eyes were solemn as his hands gently probed several firm tumor masses on her left side. When he spoke words like "specialist" and "biopsy," the patient read the unspoken thought: *malignancy.*

Mrs. Blanford was referred to Dr. O. J. Hayes. He examined her on June 29, 1959, and prescribed radiation treatment. The treatment began July 7 and was followed by surgery on September 29. After the operation, when Mrs. Blanford pleaded with Doctor Hayes for the truth, he admitted, "It *is* cancer and it's gone too far. We could not remove it because it's so widespread. One kidney is almost nonfunctioning. The pelvic bone is affected—that's why the pain in your leg. I am so sorry. I *am* sorry."

Maude Blanford was put on narcotics to control the by-now excruciating pain, and was sent home to die. Over a six-month period, while consuming $1,000 worth of pain-relieving drugs, she took stock of her spiritual resources and found them meager indeed. She had no church affiliation, no knowledge of the Bible, and only the vaguest, most shadowy concept of Jesus.

The first week of January 1960, she suffered a cerebral hemorrhage and was rushed back to the hospital. For twelve days she lay unconscious; her husband was warned that if she survived the attack it would probably be as a vegetable.

But Maude Blanford, oblivious to the world around her, was awake in a very different world. In her deep coma a vivid image came to her. She saw a house with no top on it. The partitions between the rooms were there, the furniture in place, but there was no roof. She remembered thinking, *Oh, we must put a roof on the house! If it rains, all the furniture will be spoiled.*

When she came out of the coma, Mrs. Blanford's mind was very much intact, but bewildered. What could the roofless house have meant? As she puzzled over it, a Presence seemed to answer her. Today she has no hesitation in calling Him the Holy Spirit. "He seemed to show me that the house represented my body, but that without Jesus as my covering, my body had no protection."

I leaned forward, excited by an insight: Wasn't this what I had always been taught about the Spirit—that His role was to show us Jesus and our need of him?

"At that time," Mrs. Blanford went on, "I didn't know *how* to get the roof on my house."

From then until July 1960, her condition worsened. Heart action and breathing became so difficult she was reduced from normal speech to weak whispers. Even with the drugs, the suffering became unbearable.

By July Maude Blanford knew she no longer had the strength to make the trip for radiation treatment. "On July first I told the nurse I wouldn't be coming back."

But that day, as her son-in-law helped her into the car outside the medical building, she broke down and wept. "At that moment I didn't want anything except for God to take me quickly—as I was. I said, 'God, I don't know who You are. I don't know anything about You. I don't even know how to pray. Just, Lord, have Your own way with me.'"

Though she did not realize it, Maude Blanford had just prayed one of the most powerful of all prayers—the prayer of relinquishment. By getting her own mind and will out of the way, she had opened the door to the Holy Spirit, as had happened during the period of unconsciousness in the hospital.

She did not have long to wait for evidence of His presence. Monday, July 4, dawned beautiful but hot. That afternoon Joe Blanford set up a cot for his wife outdoors under the trees. As the ill woman rested, hoping for the relief of a bit of breeze, into her mind poured some beautiful sentences:

Is not this the fast that I have chosen? to loose the bands of wickedness, to undo the heavy burdens, and to let the oppressed go free, and that ye break every yoke?... Then shall thy light break forth as the morning, and thine health shall spring forth speedily.... Here I am.

I stared at Maude Blanford over the rim of my coffee cup. "But I thought you didn't know the Bible?"

"I didn't! I'd never read a word of it. Only I knew this didn't sound like ordinary English. I thought, *Is that in the Bible?* Right away the words came: *Isaiah 58.* Well, my husband got a Bible for me. I had to hunt and hunt to find the part called Isaiah. But then when I found those verses just exactly as I had heard them—even the last three words, 'Here I am'—well, I knew God Himself had really spoken to me!"

Over the next weeks Maude Blanford read the Bible constantly, often until two or three o'clock in the morning, seeing the

Person of Jesus take shape before her eyes. It was an amazing experience, without human assistance of any kind—no Bible teacher, no commentary, no study guide—simply reading the Bible with the Holy Spirit.

Along with the hunger to meet Jesus in the Word, the Holy Spirit gave her an intense desire to be out-of-doors, close to His world. "Joe," she told her astonished husband one day, "I want to go fishing."

This made no sense to him. The terrain to the lake was quite rough. She would have to be carried down and then back up a steep hill.

But then some kindly neighbors offered to take her, and her husband acquiesced. She could not fish, of course, but she could look—at a breeze rippling the water, at the wheeling birds and the distant hills. And as she looked, a response grew in her, a response which is another of the Holy Spirit's workings in the human heart: praise. All that first day she praised Jesus for the world He had made. That night she slept like a baby.

After that, the lake trip became routine. A month or so later, Maude Blanford was walking up the hill to the road by herself. At home she had begun very slowly climbing the stairs, praising Jesus for each step attained. Or she would sit in a chair and dust a mahogany table top, saying, "Thank You, Jesus. Isn't this wood beautiful!"

Next she tried putting a small amount of water in a pail. Sitting in a kitchen chair, she would mop the floor in the area immediately around her, scoot the chair a few inches, mop again. "Thank You, Jesus, for helping me do this!"

Her daughter-in-law, who was coming over almost daily to clean house for her, one day asked in great puzzlement, "Mom, how is it that your kitchen floor never gets dirty?"

The older woman twinkled. "Well, I guess I'll have to con-fess—the Lord and I are doing some housework."

But their chief work, she knew, was not on this building of brick and wood, but on the house of her spirit, the house that had been roofless so long. Gradually, as her knowledge of Him grew, she sensed His protective love surrounding and sheltering her. Not that all pain and difficulties were over. She was still on pain-numbing narcotics, still experiencing much nausea, the aftermath of radiation.

"The will to live is terribly important," she commented to me. "It takes a lot of self-effort to get out of bed, to eat again after your food has just come up. This is when too many people give up."

One Saturday night, when the pain would not let her sleep, she lay on her bed praising God and reading the Bible. About 2 A.M., she drifted off to sleep with the Bible lying on her stomach. She felt that she was being carried to heaven, traveling a long way through space. Then came a voice out of the universe: "My child, your work is not finished. You are to go back." This was repeated three times, slowly, majestically, and then she was aware of her bedroom around her again.

The rest of the night she remained awake, flooded with joy, thanking God. When her husband woke up in the morning, she told him, "Honey, Jesus healed me last night."

She could see that he did not believe it; there was no change in her outward appearance. "But I knew I was healed and that I had to tell people." That very morning she walked to the Baptist church across the highway from their home and asked the minister if she could give a testimony. He was startled at the unusual request from someone who was not even a member of the congregation, but he gave permission, and she told the roomful of people that God had spoken to her in the night and healed her.

A few weeks later she insisted on taking a long bus trip to visit her son in West Virginia. Still on narcotics, still suffering pain, she nonetheless knew that the Holy Spirit was telling her to rely now on Jesus instead of drugs. At five o'clock on the afternoon of April 27, 1961, on the return bus journey, as she popped a painkilling pill into her mouth at a rest stop, she knew it would be the last one.

So it turned out. In retrospect, physicians now consider this sudden withdrawal as great a miracle as the remission of cancer cells to healthy tissue.

It took time to rebuild her body-house—nine months for her bad leg to be near normal, two years for all symptoms of cancer to vanish. When she called Dr. Hayes in 1962 over some small matter, he almost shouted in astonishment. "Mrs. Blanford! What's happened to you! I thought you were—"

"You thought I was long since gone," she laughed back.

"Please come to my office at once and let me examine you! I've got to know what's happened."

"But why should I spend a lot of money for an examination when I'm a perfectly well woman?" she asked.

"Mrs. Blanford, I promise you, this one is on us!" What the doctor found can best be stated in his own words:

I had lost contact with Mrs. Blanford and had assumed that this patient had expired. In May of 1962 she appeared in my office. She was two and a half years following her operation and her last x-ray had been in July 1960....

The swelling of her leg was gone. She had full use of her leg; she had no symptoms whatsoever, and on examination I was unable to ascertain whether or not any cancer was left....

She was seen again on November 5, 1962, at which time her examination was completely negative....

She has been seen periodically since that time for routine examinations.... She is absolutely asymptomatic.... This case is most unusual in that this woman had a proven, far-advanced metastatic cancer of the cervix and there should have been no hope whatsoever for her survival.

No hope whatsoever. No hope except the hope on which our faith is founded.

The miracle of Maude Blanford reminds me again of that scene on the night before His crucifixion when Jesus spoke quietly to His despairing disciples, "Ye have not chosen me, but I have chosen you..." (John 15:16). He is still saying that to us today, while His Spirit—always working through human beings—sometimes confounds us, often amazes us and is always the Guide to the future who can bring us joy and exciting fulfillment.

An Indian Jonah

W. A. SPICER AND BISHOP WHIPPLE

Not all Jonahs are in the Bible, as this pioneer story graphically reveals.

In his book, *Lights and Shadows of a Long Episcopate*, Bishop Whipple tells of an Indian helper, in the early days among the wilds of northern Minnesota, who tried, like Jonah, to run away from the call to preach the message of God to the heathen, and who, like Jonah, was sent back to the task, though not really being cast into the sea for his unfaithfulness.

Enmegahbowh was the youth's name. He had come with the missionaries from eastern Canada as helper and interpreter. He married a Chippewa maiden, who became a believer. At the time he promised her people that he would remain among them. But conditions were discouraging. The white missionaries nearest him sailed away down the Mississippi, retiring from the region. He decided to go away also, back to his earlier field at Sault Ste. Marie, on the Straits of Mackinac.

It was hard for his wife to consent to leave her people, but she said: "Enmegahbowh, I gave you a promise at our marriage. I am ready to go with you and die with you. Go, yes, go, and I will follow you." His conscience troubled him, but he decided then to go.

In the story of the attempt, told in a letter to Bishop Whipple, the young Indian tells how he and his wife journeyed to Lake Superior and there took passage in a boat. The wind was favorable. He was happy to be sailing swiftly eastward toward his own people:

O how beautiful it seemed! The captain said, "At this rate we should land at Sault Ste. Marie on the third day." With joy I said to myself, "In a few days I shall land on the beautiful shores of Tarshish, the land of my choice." The fast sailing filled my coward soul with courage. I looked to the south and saw only a small speck of land, and to the north no land.

Soon after this the wind began to fall, and the speed of the vessel to slacken. A few hours more, and a dead calm was upon us. The great vessel moved about here and there. At about five o'clock in the afternoon the sail began to move. The captain said: "The wind is coming from the wrong direction—a bad wind and always furious." At six o'clock the storm broke. The lake was white with the lashing waves, the wind increasing in ferocity. The huge vessel was tossed like a small boat, and could hardly make headway. The waves had mastered the sea, and threatened destruction in their tremendous movement.

The captain came to our cabin, drenched, and said: "We are in danger. The wind is maddening, and determined to send us to the bottom of the sea. I have sailed this great lake from head to foot for twenty-one years, but no storm has ever impeded my sailing. I have never seen anything like it. My friend, I am afraid that something is wrong with us."

He went out. His last words struck my stony heart. My dear companion saw the emotion on my face, but said nothing. In an hour the captain came again and told us of our increasing danger—that it was impossible to move ahead

and our only safety was in trying to go back to our starting place.

Nothing could be heard on deck above the rattling and roar of sails and waves, but at last the vessel swung round to go back. With difficulty we finally reached the harbor.

Before leaving the vessel, my [wife] talked with me thus: "I must say a few words, Enmegahbowh. I believe, as I believe in God, that we are the cause of almost perishing in the deep waters. I believe that although poor, God wanted you to do something for our dying heathen people. What you have said is true, that this is a great heathen country, full of darkness and idolatry."

I said, "I fully agree with your words, that I am the cause of our disaster." I had thought of this myself, but to tame down my conscience I said: "To be recognized by my heavenly Father and impeded on my journey to the rising sun! I am too small! Too poor! It is impossible!" But to her I again repeated my argument that the white missionaries, with means, education, and experience, had found it useless and had deserted, and what were we that we should do this work?

My companion asked quietly, "Do you still mean to go?"

I said, "Yes."

"I shall follow you," was her answer.

The captain said that he would start again by the first good wind. The next night at two o'clock we were again sailing at a fast rate, and again our heavy hearts were cheered. When we reached the place where we were before becalmed, the wind fell, the sails stilled, and the vessel stopped moving. A deadly calm was upon us again. There was not a cloud in the heavens. My companion and I were sitting on the deck.

An hour later, as we were looking toward the setting sun, to our astonishment and fear we saw a small dark speck of a cloud rising. My heart beat quicker. The cloud was growing and spreading. The captain cried that the wind was coming, and that it would be worse than the other.

Two hours later the sails began to move, and then came the wind and the waves with all their threatening force. The captain gave an order to throw overboard the barrels of fish to lighten the vessel. I was no longer the same man. The heavens were of ink blackness; there was a great roaring and booming, and the lightning seemed to rend the heavens. The wind increased, and the vessel could not make headway. The captain ran here and there, talking to his sailors. I thought that he was asking them to cast lots. He again said that he had never seen such a storm, and that something must be wrong on the ship, and that the storms had been sent by the Master of life, to show His power over the great world.... Again the captain cried, "Surely, something is wrong about this vessel, and we must perish."

Enmegahbowh's letter tells how the whole lesson of Jonah's attempted flight from duty came to him, with assurance that if he, too, would repent and seek God in his distress, the Lord would forgive and deliver. He does not tell how they got back to land, but by the mercy of God it was a thoroughly repentant Indian who returned; and without a doubt as to God's will, the young man and his wife set out again for her tribesmen, who welcomed them with joy. The women, he says, built a wigwam for them.

"Thus, dear Bishop," he wrote years later, in recounting his experience, "I returned to my heathen people like unto the city of Nineveh." And the bishop testifies that the young Indian became a most efficient gospel evangelist, laboring with Bishop Whipple for forty years among the Chippewas.

Of a delivering providence in the life of the young Indian's wife, the bishop says: "A providence of God may be traced in an incident which occurred many years ago, when the Chippewas were encamped on Lake St. Croix, where Enmegahbowh's wife, then a young child, was visiting an aunt. In the night the Sioux attacked the village and murdered all the inhabitants except this child, who was unnoticed as she slept between her aunt and sister. I have always looked with reverence upon this mother in Israel, whose life was spared to help and bless her heathen people."

Too Strange
to Be Coincidence

ELIZABETH SHERRILL

*Sometimes coincidences compound themselves to the point
where even the doubtingest of Thomases are forced to admit that
there has to be a Higher Power behind it all. This is just such a story.*

One winter morning in 1958, Dave Wilkerson, a skinny country
preacher, was sitting in his living room, reading *Life* magazine. He
turned a page and saw a picture of seven boys. That picture was to
change his life.

Dave was the pastor of the small Assemblies of God church in
Philipsburg, Pennsylvania. He was at home in the slow-paced rural
community; life for him, his wife, and three small children was
comfortably routine, and it probably would have remained that
way except for one thing. Dave Wilkerson had turned over his life
to God. He had simply handed over his feet and his hands and his
heart and asked the Holy Spirit to use them.

For Dave, the Holy Spirit was no vague theological term; He
was the Spirit of God, a living personality to be listened to and
obeyed. On that particular morning, looking at the picture in the
magazine, Dave Wilkerson began to weep.

It showed seven teenage defendants on trial in New York City for the death of Michael Farmer, a young victim of polio who was brutally beaten by members of a teenage gang. But it wasn't the story of the murder itself that especially gripped Dave—it was the faces of the defendants. In their eyes he saw an anger and loneliness he had never known existed. All that day he was drawn to the picture. And during the next week he felt the conviction growing that he himself—Dave Wilkerson—should take a toothbrush, get into his car, drive to New York where he had never been in his life, and try to help these boys.

At last Dave told his wife. "I don't understand why," he said, "but I must go."

It was the boldest step of obedience to the Holy Spirit that he had yet taken. Almost before he knew how it happened, Dave and Miles Hoover, the youth director of his small church, were driving across the George Washington Bridge. It was the afternoon of February 28, 1958.

In New York he parked in front of a drugstore and telephoned the office of the district attorney named in the article.

"If you want to see the defendants," he was told, "the judge himself will have to give you permission." So Dave tried to telephone the judge. He was unsuccessful. But he was not discouraged.

The next day Dave and Miles went to the trial. All morning they sat quietly, watching the seven young defendants. Toward the end of the court session, Dave hopped to his feet, ran down the aisle and stood before the bench. He knew that if he were going to see the judge at all he would have to do it then and there.

"Your honor? Would you do me the courtesy of talking with me for a few se—"

"Get him out of here," the judge interrupted brusquely.

Two guards swept down on Dave, picked him up by his elbows,

and rushed him toward the rear of the courtroom. Reporters and photographers jumped to their feet. Flashbulbs popped.

Later it was learned that the judge had been threatened by gang members and had thought the skinny preacher was one of them.

That evening the newspaper carried stories about the Reverend David Wilkerson being ejected bodily from the courtroom. As Dave and his youth director drove home, they were both depressed and confused. What kind of guidance had this been? Dave remembered biblical accounts of men who had been guided by the Holy Spirit. He'd started his own grand experiment assuming that Christ's Spirit would guide people today, just as He did in New Testament times. Why, then, was he in trouble?

At home, Dave and Miles faced a disgruntled congregation, annoyed that their minister had made a public spectacle of himself. And as the days passed, Dave's confusion increased. Not only was it difficult to explain why he had gotten into such a mess; it was more difficult to explain why, as soon as possible, he was going back to New York.

But that's where he was, the next week. When he telephoned the district attorney's office a second time he was told that if he wanted to see the boys he needed written permission from each of the parents.

"Fine," said Dave. "Could you give me their names?"

The line went dead. Dave stepped out of the phone booth. He smoothed out the now crumpled page from *Life* and scanned the caption. The leader of the boys was named Luis Alvarez. He began to call all the Alvarezes in the telephone book.

In each case the answer was indignant. No, of course they didn't have a son Luis who was a defendant in the Farmer trial!

Dave was running out of dimes with more than 150 Alvarezes to go. He gave up and stepped outside, praying, "All right, Lord. I just don't know what to do next. If this is Your business I'm on, then Your Spirit will have to show me the way."

Dave got into his car and began to drive aimlessly through the strange streets. Eventually he found himself in the heart of Spanish Harlem. Tired of driving, he parked in the first empty space he found. He got out and asked a boy if he knew where a Luis Alvarez lived.

"Luis Alvarez?" said the boy. "You parked in front of his house." He pointed to a brownstone building. "Fourth floor."

"Thank you, Lord," said Dave.

"What you say?"

Dave put his hands on the boy's shoulder. "Thank you. Thank you *very* much."

Dave climbed to the fourth floor, found the Alvarez apartment and knocked on the door.

"Come in."

He pushed the door open and saw a tired-looking man sitting on an overstuffed chair. Señor Alvarez barely looked up. "Ah, here you are, Preacher. I been expecting you. I see your picture in the paper. I say my prayers that you will come." At last Dave seemed to be getting his go-ahead sign.

Early the next morning he was back at the city jail with seven written permissions to visit the seven boys on trial.

Again he failed.

The jail chaplain, feeling that the boys were in his own spiritual care, refused to allow him entrance. Dave was crushed. "What are you trying to say to me, Lord?" he asked. "Show me where my vision is too small." He had no way of knowing that this door had to be closed in order for another—much larger—to be opened.

Suddenly a jolting idea occurred to him. Perhaps his vision *was* too small. Perhaps the Holy Spirit didn't intend him to work just for the seven defendants in the Michael Farmer trial *but for all the lonely, angry kids on the New York streets.*

Two weeks later Dave Wilkerson was back in New York. On this trip he brought with him no preconceived ideas of whom he was to help or how. He simply walked the streets, and everywhere he walked he made the same discovery: The picture of him in a New York tabloid that had seemed to Dave like a mockery of his guidance had become his entry to the street gangs of New York. Wherever he went he was recognized, "Hi ya, Preach!" from a cluster of kids on a street corner. "You're one of us, Davey!" from a tenement stoop.

Soon the churches were asking questions about this man who was "in" where they'd never even had a toehold. Fifty parishes got together and asked him to conduct a two-week youth revival in St. Nicholas Arena. Five thousand teenagers flocked to hear him. A few months later Dave had a weekly television show where teenage drug addicts, adolescent alcoholics, and fourteen-year-old prostitutes told the stories of their conversions. Eleven years ago Dave moved his family to New York so that he could minister full time to these young people. Today he directs Teen Challenge Center in Brooklyn, a home where boys and girls in trouble can come for a new start— and where the fresh paint, the curtains in the windows, and the new flower beds are largely the work of the kids themselves.

As for the seven defendants in the Michael Farmer trial, three were acquitted; four went to prison. When Dave visits them at the penitentiary, he is no longer an unknown country preacher begging admission. He is the man whose results among teenage hoodlums have people in New York shaking their heads in wonder.

As they say, it's amazing what can happen when the average man—any average man—lets the Holy Spirit be his guide.

Three Months in His Presence

VIRGINIA LIVELY

*In Scripture, we read of men and women who communed
with Him, talked with Him, face to face. But we say resignedly:
"Oh, that was back then—that sort of thing doesn't happen these days."
And, "True, the disciples were given the gift of healing,
but that gift is strangely withheld from all the people I know."*

Well, does it still happen?

❧

When friends ask how I first discovered that my hands have been given a ministry of healing, I'm sure they don't expect to hear the kind of story which I am about to set down. Apparently the fact that I am a suburban housewife who saves grocery stamps and has to watch her weight seems a poor beginning to a story of divine intervention.

It started the year my father entered the tuberculosis sanitarium in Tampa. We had long since given up hope. He was too old for an operation and we had seen the x-rays. The last thing on earth that would have occurred to any of us—Mother or my sister or me—was to ask God to step in and change medical facts.

And yet my husband, Ed, and I were active church members. As a banker, Ed was head of fund-raising. Our two children went to Sunday School and I belonged to all the groups. We were, in short, typical, civic-minded churchgoers. Which is why the tears, when they began, caused Ed and me so much embarrassment.

It was in October, as we drove home from a PTA meeting, that I suddenly began to cry. I was in charge of the Halloween Carnival that year, and at the meeting there'd been some criticism of the plans. When I was still crying at bedtime, Ed put his arms around me and said, "Honey, no carnival is that important."

But it wasn't the carnival. Even as I cried I knew that these tears were for something far bigger. I cried myself to sleep and in the morning as soon as I opened my eyes the tears started again. I choked them back, but as soon as Ed and the children left, the tears burst out again.

This incredible state of affairs lasted four days. I took to wearing dark glasses even in the house so that the family would not guess how constantly I was crying. I was sure I was having a nervous breakdown.

On the morning of the fourth day, after Ed and the children had left, a curious change took place. I saw nothing. I heard nothing. Yet, all at once there was power in the air around me. The atmosphere itself seemed to hum and crackle as though I stood in the center of a vast electric storm. As I try to put it into words it sounds fantastic, but at the time I had no sense that something beyond the possible was taking place.

I had sunk into the high-backed chair in the living room when suddenly through the window I saw the eastern horizon. Trees and houses stood between me and it, but I seemed to see right beyond to the place where earth and sky came together. And there, where they met, was a ball of light.

This light was moving, traveling toward me with incredible speed. It appeared white, yet from it poured all the colors I had ever seen.

And then it was beside me. Although it seemed impossible that anything with such energy could hold still, it took a position at my right shoulder and there it stayed. And as I stared, I started to smile. I smiled because He was smiling at me. For I now saw that it was not light, but a face.

How can I put into words the most beautiful countenance I have ever seen? *He is perfect,* was the first thought that came. His forehead was high, His eyes exceptionally large. But I could never fix the color of His eyes any more than I could the color of the sea.

More, much more, than individual features was the overwhelming impression of life—unhampered life, life so brimming over with power and freedom that all living things I had seen till that moment seemed lumps of clay.

Not for a moment did I hesitate to call this Life at my side Jesus. And two things about Him struck me most. The first was His humor. I was astonished to see Him often break into outright laughter. And the second was His utter lack of condemnation. That He knew me down to my very marrow—knew all the stupid, cruel, silly things I had ever done—I realized at once. But I also saw that none of these things, or anything I would ever do, could alter the absolute caring, the unconditional love, that I saw in those eyes.

I could not grasp it. It was too immense a fact. I felt that if I gazed at Him for a thousand years I could not realize it all.

I did not have a thousand years; I had three months. For as long as that, the face of Jesus stayed before me, never fading, never withdrawing. Many times I tried to tell someone else what I saw but the words would never come. And meanwhile I carried on with my tasks—meals and shopping and the PTA carnival—but effortlessly, scarcely knowing I was doing them, so fixed were my thoughts on Him.

At the same time, I had never seemed so aware of other people. How this was possible when my mind was full of Him alone I don't know, but it was true. My husband, especially. Far from feeling that a third person had entered our marriage, I felt that Christ *was* the marriage, as though all along He had been the force drawing us together.

And the Bible! All at once I couldn't read enough of it. It was like tearing open a letter from someone who had known this Presence as a flesh and blood person, full of just the kind of specific details I longed to hear. Certain passages in particular had a stranger effect on me: When the Bible described Jesus healing someone, the actual print on the page seemed to burn. The hand that touched it would tingle as if I had touched an electric current.

And then one afternoon before the children got home, I was sitting, just looking at Him, when all of a sudden in a patch of sunlight on the wall appeared the x-ray of my father's chest. It was all scar tissue and cavities. Then as I watched, a white mist moved slowly up the wall. When it passed the diseased tissue, there appeared on my wall a picture of a healthy lung.

"Then Dad's well!" I said aloud, and at that the Person at my side burst into peal after peal of joyous laughter, which said that wholeness was always God's way.

I thought my heart would burst as I waited for next Wednesday's x-rays. I enjoyed the scene in my mind again and again, imagining the ring of the telephone and Mother's voice stammering with excitement, "Darling—the most amazing—the most glorious—"

But when Mother called, her voice was flat. "The most annoying thing, Virginia. They got the slides mixed up! Poor Dad's got to go back for x-rays tomorrow. Why, they sent down pictures of someone who never even had TB!"

But, of course, the x-rays the next day showed no sign of disease either; Dad was healed and lived out his long life in thanksgiving to God.

And it was Dad's healing that convinced me I must try to describe the indescribable that had happened to me. I went to an elderly pastor whom I had known a long time. To my astonishment he understood me at once. He gave me some books which described fairly similar things.

Then he said the words I have wished unsaid so often.

"Don't be surprised, Virginia, if the vision fades after a time. They usually do, you know."

Fade! I thought, as I drove home with that joyous Presence beside me. *Oh, it can't, it mustn't!* For the first time in the whole incredible experience my attention veered from Him to myself. And in that instant the vision was diminished, actually disappeared for a second or two, though right away the radiant face was beside me again.

But the damage was done. The seed of self-concern was sown. The bright Presence would sometimes be missing for an hour or more. The more worried I got, the more self-centered I grew. What have I done? What will I do without Him? When He did return there would be no accusation in His eyes, just a tremendous compassion as though He realized how difficult it had become for me to see Him at all.

At last all that was left of this experience was the strange tingling in my hands as I read the Bible stories of healing. One day I was visiting a friend in the hospital. She was hemorrhaging and in pain. On an impulse I reached out and touched her. My hand began to burn just as it did during the Bible reading. My friend gave a little sigh of comfort and fell asleep. When the doctor examined her, he found that the hemorrhaging had stopped.

Over the next eight years there were dozens, scores of experiences of this kind, all as inexplicable as the first. And yet for me they were still years of emptiness and waiting. "I will always be with you," He had told me when I last saw Him.

"But how will I know if I can't see you?" I called to Him, for He had seemed so far away.

"You will see Me," He said, and then He was gone.

But the years went by and the vision had not come back. And then one day, while speaking to a church group, I saw those love-lit eyes smiling once again into mine. I looked again. The eyes belonged to a lady in the second row. Suddenly the room was full of Him; He was in the eyes of everyone in the room. "You will see Me…"

I used to wonder what would have happened if the old pastor had never spoken of the vision fading. Might I have had it forever? I think not. I think that the days when Jesus was real to my eyes were the days of the "childhood" of my faith, the joyous, effortless time of discovery. But I do not think He lets it stay that way for long.

He didn't for His first disciples; He doesn't for us today. He gives us a glimpse only. Perhaps He let me look so long because I am slow to learn. But, finally, He takes away all sensory clues. He is bigger than our eyes and ears can make Him, so He gives us instead the eyes of faith, and all mankind in which to discover His face.

They Said I Didn't Have a Prayer

GEORGE SHINN

*The accountants were in agreement: His business schools
had no chance. Best to close them right away. But then
he remembered there was one more place to turn.*

⌒〜◯〜

The five men seated at the conference table looked at one another.
Then they looked at me. No one said a word, but I could read their
minds, and what I read there made my heart sink.

I had used my last funds to hire these men, all experts in business management, to advise me on how to resolve the financial difficulties I was facing. For two hours we had been going over my
books and records. They had asked searching questions, and I had
attempted to answer them honestly.

Finally one of the lawyers—three of the men were lawyers
and two were certified public accountants—cleared his throat.
"George," he said, "would you mind stepping outside for a few
minutes? We'd like to discuss all aspects of your situation frankly
among ourselves."

Feeling like a condemned man, I waited outside. The minutes
passed slowly. Finally the door opened and I was asked to rejoin the

group. The lawyer spoke again. "I'm sorry to tell you this, George, but we can see only one solution for you. We feel you should give up and close your business schools." Give up! Here I was at age twenty-eight with my own business, and now I was facing bankruptcy.

One of the lawyers accompanied me to the elevator. I guess he meant to be kind, but his parting words went through me like a knife. "George," he said, "why don't you go to work for someone else? You don't have a prayer, not a prayer!"

I went out of the building like a man in a daze. Give up. That was all the experts could suggest. *Well*, I thought with sudden grim determination, *I'm not going to take that way out. There has to be a better way, there has to be.* But still I could hear that lawyer's voice with its mocking echo: "You don't have a prayer, not a prayer!"

The whole thing had come as such a shock that it almost seemed unreal. In the first place, I never expected to have a business of my own. When I finished high school in Kannapolis, North Carolina, my goal was to make $100 a week and to buy a new car every three or four years.

My first full-time job was as an unskilled laborer in a factory. After a couple of years I developed trouble with my back. X-rays showed an injury to my spine, probably from playing football in high school. The doctor told me I could do no more heavy work.

My mother recommended college.

I knew I needed more education, but there wasn't any money for it. My father had died when I was eight, leaving a lot of debts, and my mother had gone to work, sometimes holding down two jobs at once, to keep us going.

College seemed out of the question, but in nearby Concord was a small business college. I registered there for a two-year course.

Six months later, my savings ran out. I asked the school manager if there was any way I could earn my tuition, and he took me

on as the school janitor. For pocket money, I found a part-time job in a bakery.

One Saturday morning, I had just finished my janitorial chores and changed into my street clothes when two high-school girls came by. One of them asked, "Do you work here?"

"Yes," I said. But I didn't tell them the distinguished position that I held!

She said, "We're thinking of going to college after we finish high school. Can you tell us something about this school?"

That was easy. I liked the school. I felt I was learning important things about business administration, and I knew the school was providing a valuable community service in training young people who still were too inexperienced to get a good job in business. As I gave the girls a tour of the rooms I had just cleaned, I also told them what a great school it was. Before they left, they enrolled for the fall semester.

Monday morning, when I gave the applications to the school director, he was delighted. "George," he said, "in addition to your job as janitor, if you want to do some recruiting for the school, I'll pay you ten dollars for each student you bring in."

When you believe in something and are enthusiastic about it, you can't help but be successful. Eventually I was earning enough from recruiting to quit the bakery job. Then, when I finished the two-year course myself, the director hired me as a full-time recruiter.

I really enjoyed my work. I looked upon recruiting as more than a job. Not only was I helping the school, but I was also helping young people improve themselves and their futures. Even so, I wasn't satisfied. I wanted to become more involved in the school and feel more like a part of it. I was looking for a future myself.

One day I asked one of the owners if there was any chance that I might buy into the school as a partner. To my surprise, he said yes. We agreed on the price and that he would make deductions in my salary each week until I paid him off.

They owned three other business colleges in the state. I visited those and met the staff members and liked them. Soon I heard that the owners were ready to get out of the school business and move into other fields. With an audacity that was beyond my years and experience, I offered to buy them out.

After I took over, I soon discovered I was facing trouble. There were unpaid bills totaling thousands of dollars. On the horizon were creditors with their lawyers. Some staff members hadn't been paid for weeks, some for months. Properties were mortgaged to the hilt. I tried to get a loan at practically every bank in North Carolina, but my applications were rejected. I didn't know any people I could borrow money from. That was when I decided to have a meeting with the lawyers and accountants.

For days the words I had heard there haunted me: *not a prayer, not a prayer.* Then late one day, as I was driving home, deep in despair, I suddenly realized, "But I *do* have a prayer! It's all I have left." As a small boy I had been active in church, but when I became a little older I drifted away from it all. My faith had not diminished; I just hadn't called upon it lately.

I stopped the car along the road, and I let the words pour out of me: "Lord, You know what a mess I'm in. Everybody says I'm sunk. I don't believe You feel that way. Help me, Lord. I'm turning the company over to You. You do the guiding and I'll do the work. And anything that comes to me, Lord, I'll share with You."

A sense of great relief shot through me. I felt as though I had just been lifted out of a nightmare. I still had my problems and I still had no money. But even so, it seemed that a huge burden had been lifted.

That night I had my first good sleep in weeks. When I awoke in the morning, I felt so exhilarated that I bounded out of bed and said aloud, "Good morning, Lord!"

When I got to the office, the secretary was on the phone. She placed a hand over the mouthpiece and whispered, "It's that textbook publisher in New York. He's having a fit."

"I'll talk to him," I said. She was surprised. For weeks I had been dodging creditors on the phone and not even reading their threatening letters. I took the phone. "Good morning, Mr. Johnson," I said. "I hope you're in good health."

"Not financially," he said. "Mr. Shinn, what are you going to do about this bill of yours?"

"I'm going to pay it," I said. "In fact, I'll send you a check today. I don't know how much, but I'll send you something."

"Good," he said. "I look forward to it."

I didn't even have to open the checkbook to know that the most I could send him was one dollar, so I sent a check for that amount. A few days later, he called again and said, "Mr. Shinn, I got your check this morning. It's only for one dollar. Did you make a mistake?"

"No, I didn't," I said.

"Then are you trying to be cute?"

"I've never been more serious," I said. "I'm going to pay that bill, but you'll have to let me do it in weekly amounts I can afford. Will you go along with that?"

He thought about it, then said, "For the time being."

The next week, I was able to send him seven dollars. Gradually the bill was paid off. So were other bills, as creditors agreed to give us more time.

At first, I didn't want to tell others about my experience with the Lord on the highway, fearing that they would think I had gone off the deep end. But then I figured that if the Lord was guiding me He was probably guiding others on our team, and I decided it would be a good idea if they knew about it.

At a staff conference one morning, I said, "I think we ought to open this meeting with a prayer." Puzzled looks went around the table, followed by bowed heads. Knowing that I was going to have trouble with my first public prayer, I had written it out beforehand. And then I told them what had happened to me.

This was the turn in the road for us, as a company and as individuals, a turn to the Lord. And the answers started coming, sometimes even popping into my mind in the middle of the night. We began to reorganize the schools, expanding curriculum, increasing facilities, and trying new ideas, such as offering valuable programs for veterans returning from Vietnam. We did our best to offer first-class training in many business skills at moderate tuition costs, preparing students for successful careers in the business world.

Enrollment grew to over five thousand students; new schools were added to our chain of colleges. As our expertise increased, other schools throughout the country started coming to us for consultation services. Today the once nearly bankrupt organization has a staff of over eight hundred and serves as a management consultant to colleges in over twenty-eight states.

When I look back through the years, I'm amazed by the difference that simply turning to God and letting Him direct things has made for me. Every morning when I wake up and get out of bed, I still say, "Good morning, Lord!" because, thanks to Him, that's just what it is.

Driven Far Off Course

EDITED BY W. A. SPICER

The Methodist revival of more than two centuries ago
wrought a great work in the West Indies,
but it was not a planned revival—by humans, that is.

Dr. Coke was the agent used of God in planting the work in the West Indies. There, he was the pioneer missionary herald of the Methodist movement. He crossed the Atlantic again and again, labored in the Channel Islands, and finally, in his old age, was buried at sea on his way to plant a mission in Ceylon.

Dr. Coke gave the glory all to God for directing him to the West Indies. He had no intention of opening a work there, and he fully believed that God's providence swept him away from his own plans to do a blessed work for the vast slave populations of the islands.

His original intent was to reach Nova Scotia, where the Methodist work was to be strengthened, with a party of missionaries from England. On September 24, 1786, they sailed. Week after week storms buffeted their vessel. The seas whipped the ship's black-tarred ropes and cordage until they were frayed and white. The doctor's journal tells of precious seasons of prayer in their little cabin, where the missionaries held close communion with the Lord. But the ship could not get across the Atlantic. On December 4, more than two months later, Dr. Coke wrote in his diary: "It is very remarkable that since we came near the Banks of Newfoundland, I have had a strong persuasion, and I believe a divine one, that we shall be driven to the West Indies."

The captain, almost in despair of holding on his course, felt that the praying missionaries were somehow to blame. Crying out that there was a Jonah on board, he one day threw a lot of Dr. Coke's books and papers overboard, and threatened to throw the doctor himself over. But in the time of greatest danger from a hurricane, the little missionary party felt that God in a special way heard prayer. Dr. Coke tells the story of the experience in *The Journals of Thomas Coke:*

> A dreadful gale blew from the northwest. At ten at night I heard the captain's wife crying out in the most dreadful fright, and presently Mr. Hilditch (one of the passengers) came running and crying, "Pray for us, Doctor, pray for us, for we are just gone!" I came out of my stateroom and found that a dreadful hurricane had just arisen. The ship was on her beam ends. They had not time to take down the foresail, and were just going to cut away the mainmast as the last remedy, expecting every moment that the ship would be filled with water, and sink.
>
> My brethren and myself at this awful moment retired into a corner to pray, and I think I may say we all felt a perfect resignation to the will of God. Through grace, I think I may assert, I was entirely delivered from the fear of death.
>
> But Brother Hammet was superior to all of us in faith for the occasion. His first prayer (if it could be called by that name) was little else than a declaration of the full assurance

he possessed that God would deliver us; and his second address to God was a thanksgiving for our deliverance.

It was not till after this, and after we had sung a hymn together, that the foresail was shivered in pieces, and by that means the masts were saved, and probably the ship itself.

The captain decided to make for the West Indies, the very region to which Dr. Coke had been impressed they should go, and from this time the winds favored their journey. The sequel is told by F. Deaville Walker, of the Wesleyan Missionary Society of England in *Missionary Review of the World*, July 1914:

The God who rules the raging of the sea carried Coke and three Methodist preachers on the wings of the tempest across the Atlantic to the West Indies, and they landed in Antigua, two thousand miles from their intended destination. On Christmas morning, 1786, they landed from their half-wrecked vessel on the very island where the shipwright-preacher Baxter and his two thousand Negro converts were praying for missionaries! Coke was not the man to misinterpret such a providence or to lose such an opportunity; and as he traveled from island to island, it became still more clear that the lovely isles of the West were the appointed field. From that time Dr. Coke lived to win the Negro race for Christ. Two of the preachers he had with him were designated by conference for work in Nova Scotia. Coke promptly set aside the official appointment, and stationed his men at Antigua, St. Kitts, and St. Vincent. They may be regarded as the beginning of our foreign missionary work.

"I have no doubt but it would be an open resistance of the clear providence of the Almighty," wrote Dr. Coke from the islands, "to remove any of the missionaries at present from this country." So they were left there, to begin a work that has been a blessing indeed to that great field; for the revival of true godliness and of Bible religion, for which Methodism stood, was the reforming message of God for that day and generation.

"The Wesleyan missions," observes one commentator, "were almost the first ray of light that had come to the hopeless and benighted slave populations of the West Indies." And it was the "stormy wind fulfilling his word" (Psalm 148:8) that sent the messengers of light across the sea.

I'm Still Learning to Forgive

CORRIE TEN BOOM

*Is it possible to forgive those as evil as the Nazis, if they
had made life for you and your family such a hell?
In this story, the author of* The Hiding Place *recounts
the moment in which she was asked to do just that.*

It was in a church in Munich that I saw him, a balding heavyset
man in a gray overcoat, a brown felt hat clutched between his
hands. People were filing out of the basement room where I had
just spoken, moving along the rows of wooden chairs to the door at
the rear. It was 1947 and I had come from Holland to defeated
Germany with the message that God forgives.

It was the truth they needed most to hear in that bitter,
bombed-out land, and I gave them my favorite mental picture.
Maybe because the sea is never far from a Hollander's mind, I like
to think that's where forgiven sins were thrown. "When we confess
our sins," I said, "God casts them into the deepest ocean, gone
forever."

The solemn faces stared back at me, not quite daring to believe. There were never questions after a talk in Germany in 1947.
People stood up in silence, in silence collected their wraps, and in
silence left the room.

And that's when I saw him, working his way forward against the others. One moment I saw the overcoat and the brown hat; the next, a blue uniform and a visored cap with its skull and cross-bones. It came back with a rush: the huge room with its harsh overhead lights, the pathetic pile of dresses and shoes in the center of the floor, the shame of walking naked past this man. I could see my sister's frail form ahead of me, ribs sharp beneath parchment skin. *Betsie, how thin you were!*

Betsie and I had been arrested for concealing Jews in our home during the Nazi occupation of Holland. This man had been a guard at Ravensbrück concentration camp, where we had been imprisoned.

Now he was in front of me, hand thrust out: "A fine message, *Fräulein!* How good it is to know that, as you say, all our sins are at the bottom of the sea!"

And I, who had spoken so glibly of forgiveness, fumbled in my pocketbook rather than take that hand. He would not remember me, of course—how could he remember one prisoner among those thousands of women?

But I remembered him and the leather crop swinging from his belt. It was the first time since my release that I had been face to face with one of my captors, and my blood seemed to freeze.

"You mentioned Ravensbrück in your talk," he was saying. "I was a guard in there." No, he did not remember me.

"But since that time," he went on, "I have become a Christian. I know that God has forgiven me for the cruel things I did there, but I would like to hear it from your lips as well. *Fräulein*"—again the hand came out—"will you forgive me?"

And I stood there—I whose sins had every day to be forgiven—and could not. Betsie had died in that place—could he erase her slow, terrible death simply for the asking?

It could not have been many seconds that he stood there, hand held out, but to me it seemed hours as I wrestled with the most difficult thing I had ever had to do.

For I had to do it—I knew that. The message that God forgives has a prior condition, that we forgive those who have injured us. "If you do not forgive men their trespasses," Jesus says, "neither will your Father in heaven forgive your trespasses."

I knew it not only as a commandment of God, but as a daily experience. Since the end of the war I had kept a home in Holland for victims of Nazi brutality. Those who were able to forgive their former enemies were able also to return to the outside world and rebuild their lives, no matter what the physical scars. Those who nursed their bitterness remained invalids. It was as simple and as horrible as that.

And still I stood there with the coldness clutching my heart. But forgiveness is not an emotion—I knew that too. Forgiveness is an act of the will, and the will can function regardless of the temperature of the heart. *Jesus, help me!* I prayed silently. *I can lift my hand. I can do that much. You supply the feeling.*

And so woodenly, mechanically, I thrust my hand into the one stretched out to me. And as I did, an incredible thing took place. The current started in my shoulder, raced down my arm, sprang into our joined hands. And then this healing warmth seemed to flood my whole being, bringing tears to my eyes.

"I forgive you, brother!" I cried. "With all my heart!"

For a long moment we grasped each other's hands, the former guard and the former prisoner. I had never known God's love so intensely as I did then.

And having thus learned to forgive in this hardest of situations, I never again had difficulty in forgiving: I wish I could say it! I wish I could say that merciful and charitable thoughts just naturally flowed from me from then on. But they didn't. If there's one thing I've learned at eighty years of age, it's that I can't store up good feelings and behavior—but only draw them fresh from God each day.

Maybe I'm glad it's that way. For every time I go to Him, He teaches me something else. I recall the time, some fifteen years ago, when some Christian friends whom I loved and trusted did something that hurt me. You would have thought that, having forgiven the Nazi guard, forgiving my friends would have been child's play. It wasn't. For weeks I seethed inside. But at last I asked God again to work His miracle in me. And again it happened: first the cold-blooded decision, then the flood of joy and peace. I had forgiven my friends; I was restored to my Father.

Then, why was I suddenly awake in the middle of the night, hashing over the whole affair again? *My friends!* I thought. *People I love!* If it had been strangers, I wouldn't have minded so.

I sat up and switched on the light. "Father, I thought it was all forgiven! Please help me do it!"

But the next night I woke up again. They'd talked so sweetly too! Never a hint of what they were planning. "Father!" I cried in alarm. "Help me!"

His help came in the form of a kindly Lutheran pastor to whom I confessed my failure after two sleepless weeks. "Up in that church tower," he said, nodding out the window, "is a bell that is rung by pulling on a rope. But you know what? After the sexton lets go of the rope, the bell keeps on swinging. First *ding* then *dong*. Slower and slower until there's a final *dong* and it stops.

"I believe the same thing is true of forgiveness. When we forgive someone, we take our hand off the rope. But if we've been tugging at our grievances for a long time, we mustn't be surprised if the old angry thoughts keep coming for a while. They're just the ding-dongs of the old bell slowing down."

And so it proved to be. I had a few more midnight reverberations, a couple of dings when the subject came up in my conversation. But the force—which was my willingness in the matter—had gone out of them. They came less and less often and at last stopped altogether. And so I discovered another secret of forgiveness: that we can trust God not only above our emotions, but also above our thoughts.

And still He had more to teach me, even in this single episode. Because many years later, in 1970, an American with whom I had shared the ding-dong principle came to visit me in Holland and met the people involved. "Aren't those the friends who let you down?" he asked as they left my apartment.

"Yes," I said a little smugly. "You can see it's all forgiven."

"By you, yes," he said. "But what about them? Have they accepted your forgiveness?"

"They say there's nothing to forgive! They deny it ever happened. But I can prove it!" I went eagerly to my desk. "I have it in black and white! I saved all their letters and I can show you where—"

"Corrie!" My friend slipped his arm through mine and gently closed the drawer. "Aren't you the one whose sins are at the bottom of the sea? And are the sins of your friends etched in black and white?"

For an anguishing moment I could not find my voice. "Lord Jesus," I whispered at last, "who takes all my sins away, forgive me for preserving all these years the evidence against others! Give me grace to burn all the blacks and whites as a sweet-smelling sacrifice to Your glory."

I did not go to sleep that night until I had gone through my desk and pulled out those letters—curling now with age—and fed them all into my little coal-burning grate. As the flames leaped and glowed, so did my heart. "Forgive us our trespasses," Jesus taught us to pray, "as we forgive those who trespass against us." In the ashes of those letters I was seeing yet another facet of His mercy. What more He would teach me about forgiveness in the days ahead I didn't know, but tonight's was good news enough.

When we bring our sins to Jesus, He not only forgives them, He makes them as if they had never been.

Three

UNDER HIS WINGS WE SHALL TRUST

Are not two sparrows sold for a farthing?
and one of them shall not fall on the ground without your Father.
But the very hairs of your head are all numbered.

I've sometimes wondered who would have the audacity to decide what things, actions, mistakes, sins, or problems are quantifiable; even more do I question those who assume the prerogative of ranking them. Yet, in truth, most of us, at least to a certain extent, do just that in our day-to-day interactions, identifying with Wendy Miller in her story in this section:

> I was a Christian, and I believed in the power of prayer, but there was no way that the almighty God is going to give a hoot about something so little as soap.... There are too many big problems in the world for Him to look after. He does not concern Himself with trivial matters.

It is because of this tendency, perhaps, that many of us assume God is governed by the same human calibrations that we are: that He will agree with our rankings. If any of us *have* felt that way, perhaps the stories in this section will serve as a real jolt, for these true accounts reveal a God who regards nothing as ever being too small or insignificant to be worthy of His notice. In fact, if you study Christ's parables, you will soon discover, as I did, that He goes out of His way to challenge the societal rankings of the time, and was forever reversing them: *He that is first shall be last; he that is last shall be first.* Objects that society would consider of little worth—such as the widow's mite—He declares of greater value than a king's treasure, and the glittering gifts of the Pharisees He declares as valueless, for they come neither from the heart nor are sacrificial as compared to the widow's *all.*

These stories reflect this—that a God who would take the trouble to count each of our hairs would obviously be concerned with *every* aspect of our lives. Big or small by our judgment; that is of no consequence to Him. Under the shelter of His wings, we will find Him to be our faithful Lord of Provision.

Miracle Water

PAULA CUMMINGS

The morning was beautiful, the air crisp and energizing…
but all was not right at Pine Springs Ranch. Their water
was running out! Short of a miracle, they'd have to close camp
and send all the young people home.

༄༅།

It was a beautiful morning at Pine Springs Ranch, a picturesque summer camp nestled high in the mountains of southern California. Beams of light were sliding down the towering pines and played chase over the hillsides.

Joan stepped out of her cabin to be alone with God for just a few seconds before she would give her worship talk. Her eyes instantly caught the brilliance of the morning, and she thought, *This is a fabulous day! I can't believe how good my girls are. I can tell that God is blessing this camp already. This just has to be a wonderful week. Counseling isn't so bad after all!*

Suddenly her reflection was interrupted by a frantic voice, "Joan! Joan! Carol is in the shower all soaped up, and the water won't work!"

Joan raced to the rescue and found Carol in the bathhouse lathered up thicker than barber's foam.

"Oh, Joan," Carol sobbed, "I was taking a shower, and the

water quit, and now I can't rinse, and I'm never going to be on time for line call, and we'll lose all our merit points, and..."

"Now, Carol, calm down. There's a little trickle of water here, and we can rinse you off with a washcloth. The rest of you girls run up to the cabin and get dressed. Carol and I will be up in just a minute for worship."

With a lot of effort and a little luck, Joan straightened out the problem and rushed her cabin members to line call on time. She was still panting from all the rush when she got to breakfast. Just as she was going in the cafeteria door, she heard a familiar voice behind her and swung around. There was all six feet two inches of Larry, waist-deep in excited campers, wading through them to her.

"Hey, Joan, you sound like you've just run around the camp ten times! What's up?"

"Oh, Larry, you wouldn't believe the problems we had this morning getting everyone ready for line call! First the water quit, and my girls couldn't brush their teeth or wash, and one was all soaped up and couldn't rinse, and that's not the half of it."

"Did the water quit completely?"

"No. Good thing there was still a trickle running. The pressure must have just gone off."

"Well, maybe, but in the boys' village there is no water either—not even a trickle!"

"That's strange. Hey, I'll see you later. My girls are waiting for me at the table."

Elder Cummings, a young, vivacious man in his twenties who had an uncanny knack for dealing with kids of all ages, walked to the front of the cafeteria. "I know everyone is ready for breakfast," he said, "but I have one important announcement before we get started. I would like all the staff to come up front right after prayer for a short meeting about some urgent items."

While their campers ate, the staff gathered and waited for their director to speak. "Has anyone had trouble with the water today?" he asked.

"We sure have! Lots of trouble," was the unanimous response.

Just then Jack came bounding through the door, and Elder Cummings called him over and told the staff, "I sent Jack up to look at the spring and pump and check the water tanks. Tell us what you found, Jack."

Jack's tall, lanky frame shook as he spoke fast and excitedly, "The spring is dry. The tanks in the boys' village are empty, and the tanks in the girls' village have only about two feet of water in them. There's no way to get any more water; and if we don't get water, we'll have to close camp."

"I'm afraid Jack's right," the director said. "Staff, this is a serious problem. I know you're all shocked and as disappointed as I am, but we must not upset the campers. For the time being, just let the campers think this is a passing problem and that there is nothing to worry about. Tonight I want you all to come to a prayer meeting after you get your campers to bed, and we'll ask the Lord what to do. Until then please try to act as though nothing is wrong, and run your regular program today."

The rest of the day went fairly well, and Joan's girls didn't ask many questions about the meeting or the water. Joan had almost forgotten about the whole problem when Lynn, Elder Cummings's secretary, came up to her. "Joan, Elder Cummings wants all of you counselors to keep your kids from taking showers tonight. The lack of water would show even more then. Don't forget the meeting. When you see the other counselors, pass the word around about the showers."

Campfire time came, and the campers sang their favorite songs at the top of their lungs while Fred and John picked up the banjo and guitar. Joan's mind wasn't at the campfire bowl, though. *These kids will be so unhappy if they have to go home early,* she thought. *They're really having fun, and camp has gone so well this far. I'd be disappointed to see them go, too.*

She was brought back to reality by two hands slipping into hers as the campers stood and clasped hands to sing their nightly song of dedication.

We are one in the Spirit,
We are one in the Lord...
And they'll know we are Christians by our love...

As the music drifted out over the night air, everything seemed so perfect. Each person in camp seemed united in Christ and ready to spend a wonderful week together. Why did the spring have to run dry?

The song faded, and prayer was offered. The campers reluctantly started back to their cabins.

Joan's girls huddled around her as they made their way up the hill. Their cabin was the highest on the hillside, and no one liked to walk up the hill by herself.

"You girls will really have to speed things up tonight," Joan coaxed as she led the way into the cabin and switched on the light. "I have to go to a meeting in thirty minutes, and I want you all tucked safely in bed before I leave. So try to hurry extra fast, okay?"

"Joan," Jill tugged worriedly at her long red tresses as she talked, "Sammy said he heard Elder Cummings say he was going to close camp and send us all home because he didn't like the dumb girls. Did he say that, Joan?"

"That stupid Sammy Martin made it up, Jill, just because he hates girls," Ann retorted angrily.

"So what did Elder Cummings really say?" persisted Jill.

By this time all the girls were looking at Joan for an answer.

Joan started slowly, "Well, Jill, Sammy Martin was wrong about Elder Cummings not liking you girls, and he doesn't want to send you home. We do have a little problem, though. Remember when you couldn't get any water, Carol?" Carol nodded.

Joan continued. "Well, that's our problem. We're very low on water; and if we don't get some more, we can't keep the camp running. Don't worry though. We're having a meeting tonight about it, and we're going to ask the Lord for help. I know something will work out. Now hurry and get ready for bed; but remember—no showers, and don't use any more water than you have to."

Soon the girls were tucked into bed. Joan met Connie, another counselor, at her cabin, and they headed to the meeting together.

The lodge was buzzing with conversation when the girls arrived. Elder Cummings called the meeting to order, and everyone was seated in a circle so that the conversation could proceed easily.

"I checked into our problem a little more carefully today," Elder Cummings began. "I made a few calls and found out that this whole area is low on water. I called down to Idyllwild and asked if they could truck us up some water. They said they couldn't spare it, so I called the valley. They said it would cost us quite a bit for the amount we need, and besides that, they can't deliver for another two days because they're already bogged down with orders. Can you think of anything else we can do?"

Larry spoke up. "Elder Cummings, I think we've done everything we can do by ourselves, and we don't seem to be getting anywhere. The only thing I can see that could solve our problem is for God to work a miracle."

"I've thought and prayed a lot about this too, Larry, and I've come to the same conclusion," Elder Cummings said. "Only God can solve our problem."

Everyone agreed. Elder Cummings continued, "Let's talk to

the Lord about our situation and ask Him to provide water if He wants us to keep the camp open. Remember, the Lord knows best; and He might not answer us the way we think He should. We have to accept in faith what He knows is good for us. Let's break up in smaller groups now and earnestly pray, because what is to be done has to be done soon."

The staff members divided into small groups and began to pray as they had never prayed before. Everyone could feel the Lord's presence.

After about an hour, Elder Cummings led the staff in the camp song of dedication, "We Are One in the Spirit." At the close of the song he spoke, "Joan and Larry, it's getting late, and I hate to leave the campers alone. I wonder if you would each go back to your village to be there in case anything comes up. I know you hate to leave while we stay and pray, but you pray with us from up there."

Joan and Larry reluctantly left the beautiful prayer service. As they walked back to their villages, the feeling of God's presence went with them and they parted with a smile and the whispered words of encouragement, "God will meet our needs."

Joan prayed silently as she went from cabin to cabin checking the girls. She took extra care not to make any noise that would waken her campers. Looking around, she found all nine girls fast asleep. Joan knelt down by her bed and continued praying. When she had finished she stepped just outside to see if the other cabins were quiet. As she went back in and closed the door, a window popped open and two counselors stuck their heads inside.

"Joan, Joan, are you here?" Betty whispered excitedly.

"Yes, I'm right here," Joan answered as she ran to the window. "What's up?"

"Joan, the water tanks are overflowing—I mean, water is bubbling out the top!" Cheryl's voice quivered with great excitement as she spoke.

"It's miracle water!" Betty broke in.

"That's wonderful! When did you find out?" Joan could hardly hold her voice down to a whisper.

"When Larry finished checking the cabins in his village, he went up to look at the tanks and found them running over!" Betty related with enthusiasm.

"I've got to see this!" Joan exclaimed as she pulled on her shoes.

"I'm sorry, Joan, but you have to stay here with the kids. We're supposed to be at a thanks meeting right now. If you don't stay, there won't be anyone here. We'll tell you every detail when we get back!" Cheryl called as she and Betty started back down the hill.

Joan felt left out for just a moment, but then she remembered that it didn't matter if she saw or not—the fact was still the same. God had performed a miracle for them, for *her!* She slipped outside once more and looked up at the stars. Suddenly her heart overflowed with joy. "What a wonderful, powerful God I serve," she said aloud. "I know He cares for me and will never reject me. This is going to be the greatest camp ever!"

At that moment Joan heard some noise and turned around to see nine faces peeking out at her. She laughed and ran inside to tell her girls the story of the miracle water.

Food from the King's Table

STELLA PARKER PETERSON

*Off the southern coast of England is a very small island,
the Island of Wight, whose recorded history dates clear back
to the Roman invasion of A.D. 43. The island has long been
a vacation destination, especially for England's royal family.*

The uplands of Wight, strangely enough, are known as the
"downs," and there amid peaceful scenes many cattle and sheep
graze on the grasslands. A saying of the people is, "You can whip
our cream, but you cannot beat our milk." They are proud of their
dairy products.

Wight is a quiet isle, and its thatch-roofed cottages remind one
of a bygone day. Here lived Captain Sargeant.... His wife and his
twelve children always dreaded the days when he left aboard his
sailing vessel, and they always welcomed the days when his ship
came sailing back into harbor.

What times those twelve children must have had wandering
over the hills and playing along the beaches! But probably, as often
happens, those dozen young Sargeants looked across the water
toward the English mainland and wished they could live over there!

One time when Captain Sargeant was away on a voyage his
ship came into a great storm, and he was delayed in completing the

task he had set out to perform. The day came when he had planned to be home, and the twelve children watched eagerly for him, but when night fell, their father was still absent.

We can well imagine what earnest prayers were offered in the home that evening as the children and their mother gathered for worship. Neither was there much sleep in the Sargeant home that night. All the next day and many more days and nights thereafter, the family watched anxiously. But the ship they were straining their eyes to see did not appear. Nor did any word come from the missing father and captain.

Poor Mrs. Sargeant became very anxious, not only about her husband, but about the twelve mouths she had to feed. She was a proud woman, and said nothing to anybody about the fact that her food supplies were running low, and that she was perplexed as to where she would get more for her family. Every day she watched the food in the pantry disappear, but she did not tell her children of her anxiety.

Finally came a morning when all the food was gone. She had used the last of the flour to make bread for breakfast. Then she called the children to the table, and they all stood at their places, as they always did, for prayer. From the oldest to the youngest, like twelve stairsteps, they waited quietly, and after their mother's prayer they repeated together the Lord's Prayer. It must have sounded almost like a meeting, so many voices took part.

"Children, I have something to tell you," said Mrs. Sargeant after the amen. "This is the very last—the very last—food in the house. We have nothing to eat save this bread on the table."

Right away a junior girl spoke up.

"But, Mother, we just prayed, 'Give us this day our daily bread,' so we do not need to worry. God will give us our daily bread, because we asked Him to."

The mother had been praying earnestly, and this word from her trusting girl encouraged her as they all sat down to their meager breakfast.

While they were still at the table, someone knocked at the door. It was a friend of Mrs. Sargeant, a woman who long had been employed at the summer royal palace, where the King and Queen of England came often to entertain their friends at large house parties. In the woman's hand was a big basket.

"I hope that you will not be offended, my dear," she said to Mrs. Sargeant, "nor resent what I am about to offer you. But the King and Queen were expected last night with a large party of guests, and preparations had been made for a big dinner. But they did not come, and it seems a pity to throw away all this wonderful food. I wondered if perhaps you could not use some of it for your large family? Here is this basketful, and if the children will come with me, there is much more for them."

"See!" exclaimed the little girl of faith, "the Lord has answered us! He has sent to us not just ordinary food, but food from the King's table!"

And she gave her mother a kiss before she ran with the others down the path toward the royal residence. Back they came, a whole procession of children, carrying all that they could carry. And twelve husky girls and boys can carry a lot!

None of the Sargeants has ever forgotten how bountifully God answered their prayers in their time of need. And those twelve children, as they grew up, told the story to their children. Even to the third and fourth generations the Sargeants continue to tell that story.

Praying for Shingles

MARJORIE LEWIS LLOYD

Surely God is too busy to trouble Himself with such mundane things as shingles for a little schoolhouse. So it would seem, for day after day passed, and the school's prayers remained unanswered.

A Christian elementary school in Vacaville, California, had just been remodeled. That is, it had been remodeled except for shingles. Funds had run just that much short. And the need was serious, for the rainy season was approaching.

The children of teacher Kay Buzelli's room had memorized the words of Jesus, "With men this is impossible; but with God all things are possible" (Matthew 19:26). And they believed those words were true. For days they had prayed for shingles. And earlier that September morning, in Bible class, Kay had prayed, "Dear Jesus, please be with us today. Help us to do something to show we love others. And please, dear God, don't forget to take care of our school."

And then it happened. A sudden, great *boom!* came from the direction of the freeway, just a stone's throw away, as the tire of a giant truck blew out. Seventeen frightened children looked up to see the big truck swerve into the path of oncoming traffic. But those little people, believe it or not, did not race outside to see what

was happening. One of them said, "Let's pray that no one will be hurt." So they knelt in a circle with their teacher and prayed while the screeching, thumping, bumping, crashing sounds of a serious accident continued.

Their prayer was answered even as they prayed. The big truck had turned over and dumped its contents on the edge of the freeway. A smaller truck, in which a two-year-old boy was riding with his father, had turned over and landed in the creek beside the school. But there were no serious injuries. Even the newspapers called it a miracle.

It turned out that the miracle was even larger than it first appeared to be. For what had the big truck dumped on the edge of the freeway? Shingles! Shingles just the color needed for the school! Shingles strewn everywhere, it seemed! And nobody wanted to pick them up!

A school board member negotiated with the insurance adjuster to buy them all for a very small sum. The children picked them up and stacked them neatly. The roof was cared for before the rains, and the shingles left over were sold for a profit of $300.

Could anyone tell those Vacaville children that God doesn't answer prayer?

Faith and Four Tables

FANNY LAZZAR

She knew absolutely nothing about the restaurant business,
and not much about food—yet she decided to open her own
restaurant. She prayed, but why would the great God
concern Himself with a tiny, struggling restaurant?

I slowly lifted the shade at the front door of my little restaurant, looked at its four tables, then sank onto a counter stool, burying my head in my arms. It was 6 A.M. on a special day in 1944—my first day in business.

"Dear God," I prayed, "I don't know what to do or how to do it. Please lead. I will follow."

With two sons to support, I had borrowed capital and opened this restaurant. Yet, any businessman would have predicted my failure. The restaurant was located in an across-the-tracks area of small homes in Evanston, a Chicago suburb.

More than anything else that morning, I needed reassurance that He had put me on the right path.

I remembered when I first really learned about His help. Years of tragedy had left me convinced I was completely alone. One night in my apartment I sobbed bitterly. There was a rap at the door. It was my landlady. "Fanny," she said gently, "don't you ever pray?"

"Of course," I answered. "Always."

She put her arms around me. "But maybe not correctly," she said. "Remember that God's love has always met, and always will meet, every human need. When you pray, remember *that*, and He will never fail you."

At the time I was working in an office. However, I wasn't able to save anything for my sons' college education. And I knew I must find some other kind of work. Finally, one evening I dropped to my knees and asked God to show me the way.

The direction came some weeks later. On my lunch hour, I stepped into a restaurant advertising "Good Old-Fashioned Irish Stew." My mouth watered. But I could hardly swallow the first spoonful. It was terrible. I asked the waiter, "How can you serve this?" He glanced about, then leaned down. "Lady, I agree. It is terrible. You know why? Because the owner is greedy. He buys cheap and serves cheap."

I looked around aghast and thought, *If a person with this kind of soul can fill up a restaurant, then it seems to me someone with higher principles could do even better.* At that moment I *knew* this was His answer to my prayer. I would open a restaurant.

I didn't know a thing about the business. And I had no money.

"Lord, You have given me the will; please show me the way."

I borrowed money from friends. Twenty-five dollars here, fifty there, until I had two thousand dollars. Still not enough. Finally, a Chicago bank lent me two thousand dollars more, with two friends cosigning the note.

I rented a corner store in the poorest part of town because the rent was only fifty dollars per month. Now what would I serve? I prayed, "Dear God, I need Your guidance; *You* lead and I will follow."

Thoughts began to flow. This being the age of specialization, I felt it wise to concentrate on one or two dishes, such as spaghetti. They'd be my best.

So my adventure began. By closing time that first day, a few workingpeople had wandered in, and I shut the doors with twelve dollars in the register. I scrubbed the floor, then went into the kitchen to make sauces. As I worked, I smiled to myself; here I was, chef and owner, and yet I couldn't eat Italian spaghetti sauce! I couldn't digest it.

The thought came: Why not develop a new kind of sauce, one that would not only be easily digestible but unique in flavor? For the next fifty weeks, I spent almost every night working on it, cooking, tasting.

Finally one night I evolved a sauce made with chicken, beef, butter, tomatoes, herbs and spices. Rosa, a friend from across the street, tasted it, and looked up with shining eyes. "Ah, *fantastico!*"

Then I pencilled on my menu, "Fanny's Famous Spaghetti Sauce."

But after little over a year, I was still taking in only twelve to fourteen dollars a day serving daytime customers and had sunk eighteen hundred dollars further into debt. However, I felt in even closer communion with God and constantly turned to Him for guidance. I was given an inspiration which led to a bold decision. Instead of daytime hours, I rescheduled my restaurant to serve the evening dinner trade from 5 P.M. to 10 P.M.

Most anyone would have laughed at me. I sold no liquor. In fact, I offered no inducement except good food and reasonable prices. But I could expand my menu. Again the guidance: Why not some real southern fried chicken?

It seemed right. Only I didn't know how to fry chicken. I

advertised for a chef. Four or five men answered the ad. But they knew little more about chicken than I.

I was sitting alone in my restaurant's kitchen, praying for an answer, when an elderly man shuffled in, his white hair reflecting his years. He said his name was Bob Jordan. Love radiated from his face, but he looked too old for the job. However, to be polite, I gave him an application.

He handed it back, shaking his head. "Ma'am, I can't read or write."

"Then how did you read my ad?"

Looking me in the eye, he answered, "I didn't see any ad. I was coming down the street looking for a job and the Lord said, 'Man, open that door and enter. Your job is waiting for you there!'"

Bob Jordan got the job. And he fried the best chicken in the world!

But even with an expanded menu, I had to acquaint more people with our out-of-the-way location. Again, His help came.

I had always enjoyed writing and I began to wonder about writing a weekly column and running it as an advertisement in our local paper. I called a friend on the paper and broached the idea.

"Fanny," he chided, "no one would read it. Besides, display space is very expensive."

"What about back in the classified ads?"

"Then you'd be sure no one would read it."

"Well," I said, "I've prayed about this and I think He knows more about it than you or I."

My first column reminisced about my childhood in Italy when, visiting my uncle's farm, I'd find escape in fields of fragrant violets. "All of us need 'escape channels,'" I wrote, "and one good escape is to have a good, quiet meal alone with your husband or a friend who is dear to you." Naturally, I mentioned my restaurant.

People did read it, including a Northwestern University professor who sent a clipping to the *New Yorker* magazine, which published it as a curiosity. Soon diners were thronging to our restaurant.

Along with this success came an ever deepening awareness that all of this was possible through Him. And I learned that the only way one could really thank Him was to pass on love and appreciation to others.

Today my restaurant, which has expanded several times, is as I visualized it twenty-six years ago—checkered tablecloths, oil paintings, and books—thousands of books—lining the walls. My sons are raised and happy in their own careers. And each night, when the last guest has left and I sit alone in the dining room, I give thanks for God's blessings.

I realize that this is not my restaurant, but His. For by myself I could do nothing. But when I, in complete faith, turned to Him, He led me each step of the way.

Many people wishing to start their own restaurant ask me the secret. I tell them what He taught me, "Be more concerned with love and appreciation for others than with your margin of profit."

Or, as Bob Jordan would say, "It's the giving, not the getting, that makes the difference."

I Must Be in Quebec on Saturday Afternoon

CHARLES INGLES

*Dense fog or not, Müller was certain that
God would get him to Quebec on time.*

The well-known English evangelist, Mr. Charles Ingles, once told a story he had heard from the captain of a steamship on the Liverpool-Canadian service, with whom he crossed the Atlantic over forty years ago. It concerned the captain's experience with that man of faith, George Müller, of the Bristol orphanages.

The sea captain spoken of told his story to Mr. Ingles as the ship was creeping slowly through a fog off the Banks of Newfoundland. Mr. Ingles said that the captain was one of the most devout Christians he ever knew. The captain said:

"Mr. Ingles, the last time I crossed here, five weeks ago, one of the most extraordinary things happened, and it has completely revolutionized the whole of my Christian life. Up to that time I was one of your ordinary Christians.

"We had a man of God on board, George Müller, of Bristol. I had been on that bridge for twenty-two hours, and never left it. I was startled by some one tapping me on the shoulder. It was

George Müller. 'Captain,' he said, 'I have come to tell you that I must be in Quebec on Saturday afternoon.' This was Wednesday.

" 'It is impossible,' I said.

" 'I have never broken an engagement for fifty-seven years.'

" 'I would willingly help you. How can I? The fog has rendered me helpless.'

" 'Let us go down to the chartroom and pray.'

"I never heard of such a thing. 'Mr. Müller,' I said, 'do you know how dense this fog is?'

" 'No,' he replied, 'my eye is not on the density of the fog, but on the living God, who controls every circumstance of my life.'

"He went down on his knees, and he prayed one of the most simple prayers. I muttered to myself: 'That would suit a children's class, where the children were not more than eight or nine years of age.' The burden of his prayer was something like this: 'O Lord, if it is consistent with Your will, please remove this fog in five minutes. You know the engagement You made for me in Quebec for Saturday. I believe it is Your will.'

"When he finished, I was going to pray; but he put his hand on my shoulder and told me not to pray. 'First, you do not believe He will,' he said, 'and second, I believe He has, and there is no need whatever for you to pray about it.' I looked at him, and George Müller said this: 'Captain, I have known my Lord for fifty-seven years, and there has never been a single day that I have failed to gain an audience with the King. Get up, Captain, and open the door, and you will find the fog is gone.' I got up, and the fog was gone!"

The Miracle
of Two Blue Coats

B. LYN BEHRENS

*Dr. Lyn Behrens, president of Loma Linda University, remembers a
cold winter afternoon when finances were so tight that she had begun
to question God's leading in her family members' lives. The catalyst for
this despondency had to do with the fact that both of her daughters
badly needed a winter coat—but she had money enough for only one.*

It was cold, and getting colder by the day. Each morning the wind-
shield of the car was frosted over. At sunset little puddles in the
supermarket parking lot turned to ice. Moving from sunny southern California to Denver in the summer of 1981 had been a rela-
tively smooth transition. But as the leaves turned golden in the fall,
it was clear that our two growing daughters would need heavy
clothing for the Colorado winter. We were unprepared.

My hectic sabbatical study and work schedule didn't allow me
the luxury of crafting garments for the girls. We made multiple
excursions to the shopping malls looking for coats. Each time we
began with enthusiasm. Each time we returned with growing frustration, unable to find anything that fit them or the extremely tight
family budget.

The snow began to fall. I could delay no longer. We left home early one Sunday afternoon and drove to a Kmart south of the city. There in the children's clothing were the perfect all-weather coats—sky blue in color, lined with removable flannel, and just one of each size needed by the girls. One glance at the price tag and my relief turned to total frustration. Both girls needed a coat, but I had only enough money to purchase one.

An exhaustive search revealed no other options. Near tears, we left and drove to the local Target store. This time there was absolutely nothing that fit.

What should I do, Lord? This is not a want; this truly is a need! The reality of our changed circumstances was starkly evident in so many ways. Months before, we had sought God's leading in the career change that led us to Denver. Nagging uncertainty mushroomed suddenly into a menacing cloud of doubt. My inner dialogue continued. *God, was it really Your will that we come to the Mile-High City? Did I want to come to this research center so badly that I misread Your leading?*

On the way home we passed the Kmart again. On an impulse I swung the car into the parking lot. The girls chided me for the useless detour. We sat in the car and talked to God about our dilemma. In spite of scanty resources, we had continued to pay a faithful tithe. We claimed God's promise in Malachi 3:10-11—what could and would God do for us?

As we passed through the double doors into the store, a voice on the speaker system announced a "new special" in the children's department. It took just seconds to find the flashing blue light. There was only one item of clothing on sale—the very coats we had selected two hours previously! "Two coats for the price of one!" The garments still hung exactly as we had left them. Grabbing them, we raced to the checkout line. Even the cashier was amazed by our bargain. By the time our purchase was completed, the sale was over! In the space of five minutes our dilemma was solved. We marveled at God's amazing providence and incredible timing.

Through the intervening years the "miracle of the two blue coats" has been a source of reassurance, comfort, and courage. In times of personal and professional perplexity the story causes me to remember that God knows the details of my life and times.

Soap and Bags and Hairs on My Head

WENDY MILLER

*Wendy Miller, author of one of our most beloved Christmas stories,
"Charlie's Blanket," remembers a rainy day that matched
her inner climate. She needed vacuum bags desperately but had
only half enough money for them. If it had been a big thing,
she could have prayed about it—but the mere thought
of asking God for such a thing bordered on the ridiculous.*

Then, with her children, she listened to a story.

My kids looked forward to the 5-Day Club that was to be held in
my friend's backyard. She did it every summer. Through stories
and songs she taught of God's love. There were crafts to do, verses
to memorize and, at the end of the five days, prizes to be won.

It wasn't far and my kids knew the way, so I would just send
them out the door and then bask in the quietness that is rarely heard
when you have four small children. Usually I would clean my house,
which may sound like an odd way to enjoy yourself, but I would
have the satisfaction of seeing it stay that way for one whole hour.

One day it happened to be raining, so I drove the kids to the club. Arriving early, I went in to chat for a moment with my friend. When the rest of the children arrived I turned to go.

"You're welcome to stay if you like," she said.

I thought for a moment. Why not? I had planned to vacuum the house but I had no vacuum bags. Money was scarce these days. I had emptied the same bag and retaped it so many times that today it had finally fallen apart. I had been so frustrated and angry. Well, I would stay. It seemed I had nothing better to do.

I flopped down into a chair at the back of the room. My mind drifted back and forth between the class and my own problems. When story time began I perked up to listen. The tale was about a young boy who needed to buy soap. His clothes were dirty and he wanted to wash them, but he didn't have enough money to pay for the soap. Even the cheapest was a dollar and he only had fifty cents. So he prayed and told the Lord about his problem and asked for help. Then he went to the store, and there he found some soap that was on sale for fifty cents.

I couldn't believe my ears. What kind of junk was she trying to teach my kids! I was a Christian and I believed in the power of prayer, but there was no way that the almighty God is going to give a hoot about something so little as soap! *Look at me,* I thought. *I have only five dollars and I know that the vacuum bags are ten dollars. Kind of the same situation, but there is no way that I would bother to pray about it. There are too many big problems in the world for Him to look after. He does not concern Himself with trivial matters.* I politely waited for the hour to be up, and then I packed my kids in the car to drive home.

I was totally absorbed in my thoughts, my brain on autopilot as I drove. When I came back to the real world I realized that I had driven to the mall instead of home. I decided that wandering the mall might be a good way to spend the rainy afternoon after all.

In the mall I passed a small store that sold reconditioned vacuums. I stopped in front of it. My mind drifted back to the story. I must have stood there for a long time because the owner of the shop stepped to the door and asked if I wanted something.

I was embarrassed. "Only if you have a half-price sale on vacuum bags," I laughed. I knew he didn't. I had been there often enough to know that his prices were already low and he never had a sale on anything.

"Actually, I do in a way," he laughed in return. "A lady was just in here and somehow talked me into selling her half a package. I have the other half behind the counter. It's yours for five dollars."

I could almost hear God's voice. "Did you really think I didn't care? Don't you know that I can do anything? I care about even the smallest part of your life. About soap and bags. Even the hairs on your head are all numbered."

Wow, what a lesson! And I thought the 5-Day Club was for kids.

Feeding the Orphans

W. A. SPICER AND A. T. PIERSON

To raise large sums of money, day after day,
without a development team, without telemarketing,
without asking anyone but God for help? Surely you jest!

Few mortals have exercised greater day-to-day faith than George Müller. As an obscure pastor in the west of England, he was distressed by the general lack of faith in God among people. "I longed," he said, "to have something to point to as a visible proof that our God and Father is the same faithful God as ever He was, as willing as ever to prove Himself to be the living God."

Praying for guidance in the matter, the pastor was led to establish the work that eventually grew into the great Bristol orphanages. The enterprise truly was, as George Müller desired it to be, a testimony to the living God, who hears prayers and does things on earth.

That this might be evident to all, Müller considered it fundamental in the purpose that neither he nor his fellow workers should ask help of any man, but only of the Lord, in prayer. His thought was: "Now if I, a poor man, simply by prayer and faith obtained, without asking any individual, the means for establishing and carrying on an orphan house, there would be something which, with the Lord's blessing, might be instrumental in strengthening the faith of the children of God, besides being a testimony to the consciences of the unconverted of the reality of the things of God."

The work began in 1835. As it grew from year to year, George Müller's journal traced the record of daily dependence on God. Again and again, with no supplies for the next meal, he took each need before God in prayer, and the help came. The entry in his journal for December 1, 1842, reports ninety-six orphans in the homes, and a shortage of supplies and money. "We were unable to take in the usual quantity of bread," says the record.

Müller never laid down his own method as the rule for others. Called by the Lord to let his work bear witness to God's faithful providence, he felt only that he must never assume the burden himself. Instead, Müller was confident he must wait on God, going only so far as the Lord made a way. Day by day the Lord vindicated his faith in a wonderful manner.

At last the time came for expansion, and a building fund for new orphanages on their own ground began to come in. In 1846, Müller wrote in his journal of the experience in securing the land where the great institution was finally placed (on Ashleydown, near Bristol):

February 4. This evening I called on the owner of the land on Ashleydown, about which I had heard on the second, but he was not at home. As I, however, had been informed that I should find him at his house of business, I went there, but did not find him there either, as he had just before left. I might have called again at his residence at a later hour, having been informed by one of his servants that he would be sure to be at home about eight o'clock; but I did not do so,

judging that there was the hand of God in my not finding
him at either place; and I judged it best, therefore, not to
force the matter, but to "let patience have her perfect work."

February 5. Saw this morning the owner of the land. He told me that he awoke at three o'clock this morning and could not sleep again till five. While he was thus lying awake, his mind was all the time occupied about the piece of land respecting which inquiry had been made of him for the building of an orphan house, at my request; and he determined with himself that, if I should apply for it, he would not only let me have it, but for one hundred and twenty pounds per acre instead of two hundred pounds, the price which he had previously asked for it. How good is the Lord! …Observe the hand of God in my not finding the owner at home last evening. The Lord meant to speak to His servant first about this matter during a sleepless night, and to lead him fully to decide before I had seen him.

As the orphanages filled up, until more than two thousand children were being cared for at a time, still it was a work of daily waiting on the Lord for supplies. Day after day closed with no balance in hand, but with each day's absolute necessities met. While the Lord supplied their needs so wondrously, Müller was an economist, conscientiously saving what he could. He felt that only so could he expect God to hear and answer.

During this time of his own need, Müller also prayed on behalf of foreign missionaries in that time of missionary expansion in far lands; and many gifts were sent him for this work and for Bible distribution. He writes of the help he then sent to the missionaries: "It has frequently, yea, almost always, so happened that the assistance which God has allowed me to send to such brethren has come to them at a time of great need. Sometimes they have no money at all left. Sometimes even their last provisions were almost consumed when I have sent them supplies."

In a summary of this man's life by Dr. A. T. Pierson, it appears that Müller, a poor man, had in sixty years been enabled:

1. To build five of the largest orphanages in the world, in which over ten thousand children were cared for.
2. To give to school work over half a million dollars.
3. To circulate nearly two million Bibles and portions, and three million books and tracts.
4. To give over a million and a quarter dollars in aid of missionary work in various lands.

Altogether, in the sixty years, this man, without personal resources, who had less than three hundred dollars when he died, had had put into his hands to distribute about seven million, five hundred thousand dollars.

Truly the Lord helped George Müller to leave the witness, according to his desire, that God is the living God.

Four

HE SHALL GIVE HIS ANGELS CHARGE OVER US

Be not forgetful to entertain strangers: for thereby some have entertained angels unawares.

HEBREWS 13:2

Of all the Angel stories, none are treasured more than these, for the experience of actually *seeing* a celestial being occurs so rarely that when it does, it can never be forgotten. One may hear words spoken by an angel, one may experience the presence of an angel, or one may be spoken to by an angel in a dream—but none of these experiences, as wonderful as they may be, can possibly equate with having seen one. The very thought of having come this close to a being from another world, more specifically, from heaven itself, is enough to send chills up and down one's spine.

Perhaps most face-to-face encounters that we know of (at least in our time) could be best, and most characteristically, capsulated in Veldonna Jensen's story:

There before her stood a man! He was smiling, and his handsome face seemed to be lit up with kindness. "Are you afraid, little girl?" he asked.

"Yes," she answered.

The kind stranger said, "Do not be afraid any more."

A great calmness filled Sue's heart, and all her fears suddenly disappeared.

Kindness: the one quality that, more than any other, radiates from God's throne through His angels. It is a defining quality—without it, the being cannot possibly have come from God's throne; with it, the being almost certainly cannot have come from the Father of Evil.

Gun in His Hand and Murder in His Heart

A NARRATIVE
OF EARLY AMERICAN TIMES

*The threat of death: That was what awaited Lutheran pastor
C. G. Steinhofer as he passed through a wood back when
America's eastern settlements were called the "frontier."*

⟨flourish⟩

In his pastoral labors it came to Steinhofer's knowledge that a
member of the congregation was living a double and wicked life.
He labored with the man, but to no avail. Then he told the
offender he would have to rebuke the man's sin publicly.

The man threatened the pastor, and finally, just before the
public service, gave him notice that he would surely do him vio-
lence if he made the matter public. The pastor, however, discharged
his duty, and called on the congregation to pray that the evil might
be removed from their midst. The offender was so enraged that he
immediately prepared to take the pastor's life. Knowing that he
would pass through a wood to visit a sick member, the furious man
lay in wait for the minister, with a gun in his hand and murder in
his heart. The narrative continues....

In due time the clergyman came in sight; but to the dismay of the watcher, two men appeared to be with him, one on either side. This, for that time, baffled his intention; but being determined to effect it, he concluded to do it when the visit was over, and therefore remained waiting in the wood. Steinhofer, after a short period, returned, but to the surprise of his enemy, the two men who had appeared to accompany him as he went were still apparently beside him; and thus he again passed safely through the wood, not knowing that it concealed an enemy.

Perplexed in mind and uneasy in conscience, the offender felt an earnest desire to know who the men were whose presence had protected his intended victim. To obtain that knowledge, he sent a servant maid on some trivial errand to the house of the minister, telling her to find out who the strangers were who accompanied him on his afternoon visit. She made inquiry, and was told that he went out alone, and took nothing with him but his Bible, which he carried under his arm.

This return to his question startled the man more than ever. He immediately dispatched a messenger to the clergyman, demanding who those two men were who, one on his right and the other on his left side, accompanied him to visit the sick man. The messenger was also instructed to say that his master had seen them with his own eyes.

C. G. Steinhofer, although he knew not what peril he had escaped, yet felt convinced that the Lord's hand was in the thing, and also that He had, by His preserving providence, been round about him that day. He bade the servant tell his master that he knew of no man having accompanied him. "But," he added, "I am never alone; the Lord whom I serve is always with me."

This message, faithfully delivered by the servant, produced a powerful effect on the master. His conscience was alarmingly awakened. He immediately complied with the requisitions of duty, and the next morning, as a humble penitent, he called on his faithful reprover, with tears confessed his past crime, and also disclosed his wicked intention so providentially frustrated.

Aunt Emma's Angel

FLORENCE COLEMAN

Fay posed a question out loud she had wondered about for a long time: "I'm just wondering—are the days of miracles over? We never hear of any now."

In answer, Aunt Emma told her a story.

❧

Fay was curled up on the large sofa, idly looking at the pages of her book. But her thoughts were far away from the things revealed in the book. Why was it that nothing wonderful happened to God's people now, such as happened to them back in Bible times? She wondered.

Aunt Emma, who had been reading stories to seven-year-old Wayne, looked up and noticed the troubled expression on Fay's face.

"What seems to be the trouble, dear?" she asked.

Fay smiled. *Aunt Emma is such a dear,* she thought to herself.

"Well, I was just thinking over some of the things Pastor Brown talked about at church this morning. You remember he told of the way God cared for His people and protected them all through their wanderings in the wilderness. And he mentioned that in Bible times the sick were healed, the lame made strong, and some were even raised from the dead. It was wonderful! Miracles were performed ever and ever so many times. Of course, they were all done for the glory of God, but I am just wondering—are the days of miracles over? We never hear of any now."

"The very same God who heard the prayers of men like Abraham, Elijah, Elisha, Moses, Peter, and Paul, and many others, is just as ready to answer our prayers today. He supplies—"

"Yes," Fay interrupted, "but I haven't heard of many people being miraculously healed, protected, or raised from the dead within my lifetime."

"I believe that God's wonderful saving grace and power are manifested around us every day," continued her aunt positively. "Perhaps it is our own fault that we do not recognize these happenings as miracles."

"What do you mean, Aunt Emma?"

"I mean that every day, somewhere, someone is being protected or helped in a special way by our heavenly Father. Would not you call it a miracle if you were about to lose your life and were saved from death in a remarkable way?"

"Well, yes, I would," answered Fay, with a note of doubtfulness in her voice.

The sun had edged its way behind the western hills, casting a dull-red glow over the whole room. The light made Aunt Emma's face look like the face of a girl eighteen years old rather than that of a woman thirty-six, as she asked thoughtfully, "Did anything ever happen to you that made you feel as if a real miracle had been performed for you?"

Fay tried to look interested. Her aunt went on talking, without waiting for an answer to her question.

My mother, your grandmother, was once very ill. This particular afternoon she seemed to be getting worse instead of better.

We lived three and a half miles from the little town of Saxonville. Our nearest neighbor lived four miles beyond us. We had no telephone; so my father decided that I should go to town for the doctor. One look into my mother's white face, and I knew I had to hurry.

I ran out the back door and started through the field. The ground was rough and stony, which made it hard for me to run very fast. I finally came to the railroad track. There I paused to decide which way to go. If I followed the railroad track, I would reach town much more quickly than if I followed the highway. Just the remembrance of father's anxiety and of mother's white face there on the pillow was enough to settle the matter. But I had not heard the three-thirty freight train go by. Quickly, I decided that it must have passed while I was in Mother's room talking to Father, for that train was never late.

I ran as long as I could; then I slowed to a walk as I came to the trestle that crossed the river bed. For a moment, as I looked at the length and the height of the trestle, I shook with fear, but I could not turn back. Over and over I thought, *Oh, what if Mother should die while I am gone?* I think I ran a little, but it seemed as if the railroad ties were either too far apart or too close together for me to land on them while running, so I slowed down to a walk.

When I was just about in the middle of the trestle, my shoestring came untied. I wished with all my heart that I could wait to tie it until I was over on the other side of the river. I walked only a few steps, but decided I would have to stop then and there and tie that shoestring. As I stooped down, I thought I heard a train whistle. A sudden terror filled my heart. I stood erect to listen. Again it came—piercingly clear—that *whoo-oo!* of the approaching fast train. The three-thirty freight had been delayed and was making up time.

I stood paralyzed with fear. It was coming closer and closer. What should I do! It was too far to jump, and I knew that I would only be racing with death if I turned back. Why had I ever taken such a chance when Mother had warned me so many times about the danger of crossing the old trestle? Would Mother die if I couldn't get the doctor? Why hadn't I been sweeter to brother that morning? He was a dear little boy. I didn't want to die! But I felt sure that that long freight would soon crush me to death!

All these thoughts flashed through my mind in a second. My feet seemed glued to those ties. Again the whistle sounded. It was louder and more shrill this time. In another moment the engine would round the curve!

I closed my eyes and breathed a prayer for help. When I opened them, there was a man coming toward me. He said, "Little girl, don't turn back. Run, and you will be able to get clear of the track in time!"

Instantly I obeyed the tall, clean-looking man and ran with all my might. My shoe got looser, and finally I kicked it off to keep from stumbling.

The train rounded the corner of the hill. It was coming nearer. Each time I lifted my feet they seemed to get heavier. Would I ever make it? When I reached the end of the trestle, I gave one leap to the side of the track, and the train rushed onto the bridge. As the freight cars rolled by, I cowered on the cinder bed by the side of the track.

When the last car had disappeared, I went back to get my shoe, which had stuck between the ties. I could see it from the end of the trestle. As I stooped to put it on, I suddenly remembered the stranger who had saved my life. Where could he have gone? He certainly hadn't had time to beat the train to the other end of the trestle. I wanted to thank him. Where was he? This thought worried me as I ran on to town for the doctor.

On our way home, the doctor, to whom I had told my frightful experience, suggested that we look for this stranger. We both watched at every crossroad, but we saw no glimpse of him.

As soon as the doctor had done all he could to make Mother comfortable, he related the story of my experience with the stranger to my father. All agreed that this must have been an angel—perhaps my guardian angel!

Tears of joy filled my father's eyes, as he said in quiet tones, "God cares for each one of us."

We knelt there by Mother's bed and thanked our heavenly Father for His protecting care.

The story was ended. Fay looked up into her Aunt Emma's face. Doubt no longer clouded her eyes. They shone with faith and trust as she said, "Aunt Emma, you are right. Miracles *are* still being performed, only sometimes our eyes are blind to them."

The Angels of Chortiza

GWENDOLYN LAMPSHIRE HAYDEN

*They were lost in the maze of the forest, and at any moment
their enemies might discover them. They were slowly dying
of starvation, and the cold was unrelenting. If they did not
somehow escape by this night—it would be too late.*

Eduard crouched miserably in the back of the lumbering wagon
and wondered whether he would ever again be warm. All day he
had stumbled along with the tired group of men and boys who
waded through the drifting snow in order that the women and
children might find room on the already overcrowded cart. It was
not until late afternoon that he had fallen face downward into one
of the deeper drifts. Dully he recalled that he had lain there exhausted until Gerhard had lifted him up and had pushed him into
the tiny space between Mother and Amalie and little Lina.

"No, no, I cannot ride," he had exclaimed thickly and with
great effort. "This wagon is for the women and children. I am not a
child. I must get off and walk with the men."

"You must ride, Eduard." As from a great distance he heard his
kind brother-in-law's voice. "It has been many days since we have
found any food to eat. All this time you have been walking. But
now you are too weak to stand on your half-frozen feet. Because I

once was strong I am able to keep on. But unless help comes soon I, too, will fall into the deep snow. Unless tonight we find our way out of this forest we shall all die!"

"What is wrong, my little brother? You are not ill?" He heard the quick voice of his sister Eliesabet and saw the white blur of her thin face as she turned from the wagon seat and looked anxiously in his direction. He knew that her tired eyes could not find him among the mass of refugees crowded together into this clumsy wagon that had so miraculously fallen into their hands. Feebly he lifted his hand above his head and waved.

"I am all right, my sister. Do not worry about me. Think only of the three little girls. They must be cared for. I am old enough to look out for myself."

The boy saw the despairing droop of his sister's shoulders and knew that she, too, was weary to the point of exhaustion. But well he realized that for them, as for the thousands of other displaced and now homeless people, there could be no rest. Neither by day nor by night could there be any rest from the enemy pursuit. Nor could there be any safety unless they soon found their way out of the dense forest in which they had become so helplessly lost.

As he slumped against the side of the rough wagon he thought wistfully of the long-ago days when his father had been home. Then their life in the five-room white brick house had been a pleasant one, for Father and Mother had both been well and strong, and together they had made the home a happy dwelling place. In those times they had all gathered together each morning and each evening for worship and Bible study—Father, Mother, Eduard, and the three older brothers, who had later been taken away by the invading army.

He recalled how all of them had loved the Bible. He remembered how eagerly they had searched the pages of the Holy Book for the precious truths hidden therein, even though their study had been done in secret behind the heavy wooden shutters of the double-paned windows. For in those times they dared not let it be known that they were Bible students, lest the soldiers come in the middle of the night and take away the men of the household.

Eduard's head dropped forward on his chest, while in a half-dream he relived the years since he was a small boy at his home in the little village on the broad, fertile plains. Again he heard the cries of his playmates as they ran merrily about in their childish games. Again he watched his father as he left early in the morning to work in the factory that was nearby.

He groaned as in memory he smelled the good odors of his mother's savory borscht. Hungrily he pictured its tiny, tender slices of potatoes, cabbage, carrots, onions, and tomatoes floating temptingly in the rich sour-cream liquid soon to be ladled into their waiting soup bowls.

Hunger cramps cut through his empty stomach with knifelike sharpness as he recalled the delicious, nose-tickling fragrance of the loaves of crusty whole-wheat bread baking on the iron grate thrust over the glowing coals in the huge, built-in stone stove.

His ice-cold flesh throbbed painfully as once more he felt the comforting rustle of the straw mattress and the warmth of the feather-bed covering on the pull-out bench beds near the big heater. He remembered that it was here that he and his brothers had slept snug and warm through the winter temperatures of thirty to forty degrees below zero.

He shuddered as he thought of the dark, stormy midnight when the dreaded knock at last sounded on their door. Hot tears again burned against his eyelids as with remembering ears he heard his mother's frightened whisper, "Who's there? Who knocks at the door of Herr Heinrich?"

Eduard winced with the recollection of the harsh voice of the officer who had cried demandingly, *"Othrewaj dweri"* ("Open the door immediately"), and then had tramped unbidden into the shadows of the warm, candlelit kitchen.

"Where is the man of this household? And why has he been teaching the people to turn against the government?" the officer had thundered, his fierce eyes glaring at the terrified family.

"I am the head of this household," Eduard had heard his father say bravely. "And I am guilty of no wrongdoing against the government. All these years I have worked hard to provide food for my growing family. Not once in all the long years since our ancestors came here from Holland has one of us been disloyal in any way to this country of our adoption. Ever have we kept to ourselves and tried to be good and law-abiding people. Ever have we tried to teach our children what is right and just."

"The man speaks mighty words," the officer had sneered, and Eduard had seen his thin lips tighten in anger. "But in them is there no truth. Indeed, Herr Heinrich, it has been reported that for some time have you been showing pictures—strange pictures of terrible-looking beasts that come up out of the earth. Surely this can be nothing but a plot against our government."

"Pictures of beasts, you say?" Eduard had heard his father ask quickly. "Ah, it is concerning those that you question me in the middle of the night. Come to the table. By the light of the candle I will show you my Bible charts, for it is of them that you speak. Here. See with your own eyes how I have drawn them from the prophecies of the Bible. I assure you there is nothing here that is in any way directed against this or any other earthly government. There is here only a pictured story of Bible history."

"You dare to speak of the Bible and yet tell us that you are not against our government?" the enraged officer had roared. Eduard had seen him clench his fists until the veins stood out against the whitened knuckles. "For one crime alone would you be exiled, but now you are guilty of two crimes. For this you shall be banished immediately."

Eduard had heard his mother's stifled moan and his father's quick indrawn breath.

"Where you are going you will have ample time to think upon your treason. Come. Now there is no time to waste. With us you shall go this moment."

"No, no. This cannot be." Eduard had felt his eyes sting as he added his boyish, pleading voice to his mother's pitiful cry. "We have done nothing to deserve this. I swear to you that we are guilty of no wrong. Only let my father stay with us. Without his help we cannot earn enough to eat, for already the armies are taking away our crops. Let my father remain, I beg you."

He had seen his mother fall back hopelessly as the angry officer replied to them in scorn. "Save your words, boy. Speak no more. Herr Heinrich goes with us. Let this be a lesson to all the boys in this village lest they too grow up to meet the fate of this man. And now we leave. There is no time to spend in idle good-byes. Put on your coat and warm cap, Herr Heinrich. These you will need where you are going, I can promise you."

The sound of the soldier's coarse laughter had mingled with his mother's heart-broken cry and had blended into a sound that ever afterward Eduard was to hear in his frightened dreams. Ever afterward that dreadful night marked for him the beginning of a long reign of terror: his innocent father dragged away in the midnight hour, never to return; his three brothers taken away into the army and lost to their loved ones; the dreadful bombardment of the town where he had gone to live with his sister Eliesabet and her husband,

Gerhard, when gaunt hunger had crept across the land; the eleven-day train flight over the steppes, wedged like dumb beasts into cattle cars; the horror of the two long years in the refugee camp.

The nightmare years merged together into the sharp reality of the present flight from their two-year stay in the land where they had sought asylum. Eduard opened his eyes, keenly aware of the horror of their escape before the advancing army, some of whom were even now pressing close behind them. He saw his mother's gray head bent forward upon her chest, and he prayed as he had never prayed before that somehow God would lead them out of this forest and spare their lives.

He knew that she could not stand many more days of hunger and fear. Already she and her daughter, Maria, and her daughter's children had traveled hundreds of miles from home to be reunited, almost as by a miracle, with Eduard and his sister's family. Together the little band had pressed forward, joined by other despairing refugees, until now their wagon was crowded to overflowing with its thirty-two passengers.

He listened to the heavy breathing of the two exhausted horses and the dismal screech of the wagon wheels as they plowed slowly through the fresh-fallen snow. He shivered as the wintry northern wind cut through his thin clothing and slashed into his quivering flesh. Again the keen pangs of hunger gripped him as he tried dully to recall how many days it had been since he had had any food.

But I mustn't think about that, he thought despairingly. *I mustn't. I've got to be strong and brave, so that I can help my sister with her three little girls. Already the weather has become so cold that baby Anni has almost frozen in the little nest of straw that we have made for her here in the wagon. Soon it will be night, and we will be unable to travel any farther, for we are lost. Some of us who are stronger will have to stay awake and seek for some way out of this forest, else we will all perish and the wolves will pick our bones clean and white.*

Already Gerhard has told me that our lives depend upon finding our way to safety this very night. And he has said that without the Lord's help we are doomed to die. Indeed, I know well that we cannot live through the bitter darkness without food or shelter of some kind, for it has been days since we have eaten or rested.

"O God," he prayed, "I know that Thou dost still watch over us. I know that Thou has spared our lives and brought us this far in our flight from danger. May our guardian angels be by our sides and lead us in safety from this dense forest. Answer our prayers, O God. Answer our prayers, and we will give Thee all the glory and honor forever. Amen."

"Listen."

Eduard raised his head, startled by Gerhard's low voice. He saw that everyone else had also roused and that every face was turned fearfully toward the right, listening, listening to the distant sound borne on the rising wind.

"O Gerhard, what is it?" he heard Eliesabet gasp. "Is it—do you think the soldiers—oh, what shall we do! What *shall* we do!"

"I know not what it is, but I fear for the worst," he heard Gerhard's slow reply. "Yet there is nothing that we can do but continue to pray. Let us stop and lift our hearts to God. Let us ask that His protecting hand may be stretched over us to blot us from the sight of our enemies and to lead us from this great forest.

"Surely the beautiful words of the Psalms are as true today as in the days of old, for we know that the same God rules yesterday, today, and forever. He has promised that 'He shall cover thee with his feathers, and under his wings shalt thou trust.... Thou shalt not be afraid for the terror by night...Nor for the pestilence that walketh in darkness.... There shall no evil befall thee, neither shall any plague come nigh thy dwelling. For he shall give his angels charge over thee, to keep thee in all thy ways. They shall bear thee up in their hands, lest thou dash thy foot against a stone.' But let us continue to trust our God, Eliesabet. Then, come what may, we shall be in His care and keeping. And now, loved ones, let us pray together before we press onward in the gathering darkness."

Eduard never forgot the majestic sound of the Lord's Prayer as it arose from the pale, chilled lips of the weary refugees who pressed close together and humbly bowed their heads.

"Unser Vater im Himmel! Dein Name werde geheiligt!
Dien Reich komme. Dein Wille geschehe auf Erden
   wie in Himmel.
Unser täglich Brot gib uns heute.
Und vergib uns unsere Schulden, wie wir unsern
   Schuldigern vergeben.
Und führe uns nicht in Verschung, sondern erlöse
Uns von dem übel. Denn dein ist das Reich und die
Kraft und die Herrlichkeit in Ewigkeit. Amen."

He never forgot the earnestness of the weak voices as they prayed in utter faith and asked that God would that very night lead them to safety and to shelter. And he never forgot the shock of Gerhard's hoarse, unexpected call at the conclusion of their brief prayer meeting.

"Halloo, I say!" Again he heard his brother-in-law's voice. "Who are you, stranger, and can you help us? For we are hopelessly lost in these woods and cannot make our way to safety."

In the gathering dusk Eduard strained his eyes to see to whom Gerhard was pointing. A thrill ran down his back as he saw the dim outlines of two men, each seated on a white horse, each waiting silently for the wagon to move close to them. He noted wonderingly that the beautiful animals stood as though carved in white marble until, in response to some unseen signal, they moved forward with a silent fluid motion unlike any he had ever seen.

"Wait, strangers. Can you show us the way? Answer me, I beg of you." Again he heard Gerhard's imploring question. Again he saw the white horses stop and then move slowly forward in one common impulse. Their movement was the only answer to Gerhard's question, for their silent riders did not speak but only pointed straight ahead.

"Are you going to follow where they lead us?" he heard his sister ask fearfully. He sensed the tearful note in her voice, and knew that she feared possible betrayal into the hands of the enemy. "O Gerhard, stop. Perhaps this is a trap, and we will all be captured and killed," she half sobbed.

"Then it is a chance that we must take, Eliesabet," came Gerhard's low reply. "The little children and the older people will freeze to death if we stay here another night, for we have no warm clothing and no bedding. They cannot endure this biting cold or the cruel pangs of hunger for many more hours.

"But somehow I cannot believe that this is another trick of the enemy. Somehow I cannot believe that God will permit us to die after leading us this far. Deep in my heart is the conviction that these men wish us well and that they will help us. Let us continue to trust in God and to pray that He will deliver us from 'the snare of the fowler.'"

Eduard noted the sudden silence that fell upon the group of weary, homeless ones pressed close against him. No one spoke aloud, but all prayed silently as the thin, tired horses labored through the night. Again the exhausted children slept as the worn wheels creaked against the glittering snow crystals that sparkled in the light of the newly risen, cold, pale moon.

On and on through the long night hours the pilgrimage wound its way among the trees. On and on they rode, unquestioningly following the white-robed horsemen just ahead. Wonderingly Eduard noted that no sound betrayed the movement of the beautiful white animals. Wonderingly he saw that no steaming breath could be seen ascending from their flaring red nostrils.

On and on and on. Eduard marveled at the sure, steady guidance of the strangers. Well he knew that none of his refugee party could have found his way from the maze of trees into which they had fled in their headlong escape. And well he knew that without the help of these kindly strangers his forlorn group was doomed to die. He tried to think how far they had come in their long flight from fear—how far—how very far—how very, very far....

"Pr-r-r!" ("Whoa!")

Eduard roused with a jerk and stared wildly about him. He saw that in the east the first faint red light of the dawn was painting the cold gray sky and touching the white sleeping world with that mysterious light for which there is no description. His sleepy eyes looked back at the green forest crowding close behind them and then ahead at the two white horses standing directly in front of their wagon. He listened to Gerhard's excited voice as he turned and urged the passengers to wake.

"Look, friends," he cried joyfully. "At last we are out of the dreadful woods. At last we are on our way to safety, far from the pursuing soldiers. All night have these kind strangers led us through the deep forest. All night have they led us to this very spot and pointed ahead to a path that is safe for travel.

"Indeed, they have even led us to food and shelter, for close behind us is a hurriedly deserted house. And in it has one of our group found not only loaves of bread and a large can of syrup but also some torn quilts, which we can wrap around the children and the old folks.

"Truly, we can never thank these men enough for their great goodness. But at least we can try to do so, each and every one of us."

Quickly Eduard once again turned his eyes toward the silent, mysterious riders and prepared to call out the thankful words that pressed against his lips. But the message died unspoken, and he felt weak and breathless and half-afraid as he stared about him. For, though he looked in every direction, he could see no trace of the two white horses or the two riders who had only a moment before rested in front of their wagon.

"Quick, Gerhard," he gasped. "Be quick. The men have gone. Oh, where could they be? Why, they were standing right there as you began speaking. I saw them as plainly as I see you, and *you* haven't vanished.

"Surely they must have turned to the left and again entered the forest. Let us hurry to catch up with them and give them our heart-felt thanks. We must tell them of our gratitude."

Eduard knew that he would never forget the strange feeling of awe that swept across him as he saw Gerhard's weary face begin to glow with light and warmth.

"'He withdraweth not his eyes from the righteous.... He delivereth the poor in his affliction,'" Eduard quoted solemnly, triumphantly.

"Surely the Lord has been in this place, and we knew it not. All night long we have traveled through a forest infested with soldier spies. Many times I saw the glow of a distant campfire and heard the roar of rough laughter. Yet not once were any of those soldiers permitted to hear the sound of our creaking wagon or the laboring breath of our almost exhausted horses. Surely our guardian angels who were by our side in our home have been with us all along the way.

"Are we not told to 'be not forgetful to entertain strangers: for thereby some have entertained angels unawares'? Truly this day our eyes have beheld a miracle!"

And as Eduard looked from Gerhard's face to the fresh, unbroken snow that lay spread out in front of them, he knew that on this morning those Bible truths had once gain been fulfilled. He knew that God had indeed sent His angels to lead them in safety so that their lives might be spared. And in his heart he determined anew that, come what might, he would always be faithful to the One who had so miraculously delivered them.

The Angel of the Lord

VELDONNA JENSEN

*Never could she feel safe again, Sue decided. Not after
that awful man—with low forehead and fierce black eyes—
had broken into their house and stolen their most valuable things.*

*And now Mother was asking her to stay there on the isolated ranch
again—alone? Her eleven-year-old body started trembling
like an aspen tree during a storm.*

The old weather-beaten wagon creaked away down the grass-grown trail that led out over the prairie. The dazzling rays of the early morning sun gave promise of a warm summer day.

"Good-bye!" called Sue from the doorway of the little sod house. A chorus of good-byes echoed from the departing wagon. She watched until the family had disappeared, thinking all the while how she would have liked to go to Sabbath School with them. However, it was seventeen miles to the little country church, and they wouldn't get back till late. Someone must take care of the hundreds of baby chickens at home, and it was her turn to stay.

Turning from the doorway, she went into her mother's bedroom and stood before the only mirror that the family possessed. There she combed and braided her long black hair—somewhat of a feat for an eleven-year-old girl! She didn't like those big brown freckles on her nose, but pioneer girls didn't have such luxuries as face powder and freckle cream.

After feeding and watering the chicks, Sue curled up in the big rocker and began to read her Bible. The long day dragged on. She grew tired of reading, watching the chicks, and playing the old mellow-toned organ.

Late in the afternoon Sue went to the door for about the tenth time to see whether her parents were coming. She wasn't afraid, but she was getting lonesome. To her surprise a short, stocky man was coming down the trail to the house. Strangers were seldom seen out there on the prairie. She didn't like the appearance of this one. He had fierce-looking black eyes and a low forehead. As he strode up to the door, Sue courageously spoke:

"Good afternoon, sir."

There was no answer.

"What can I do for you?"

He only pointed to his ears and his mouth, conveying the idea that he could neither hear nor speak.

Seeing that she did not call her father or mother, the visitor at once took in the situation and realized that she was alone. He brushed her aside and walked into the house. He had with him a large canvas bag into which he began stuffing Mother's good silverware, the linen tablecloth, Father's work boots, Charlie's new jackknife, and some of Sue's own things.

By this time Sue was too frightened to stand still. As she bounced out the door, she heard him shout roughly at her. This terrified her still more, since he had pretended that he could not speak.

Not stopping to look back, she fairly made the dust fly in her haste to get away from the house. She ran and ran until she thought she couldn't take another step. However, she was afraid to stop and afraid to look back. Soon she heard the creaking of the wagon and the sound of voices in the distance. Yes, here they came at last! Faster and faster sped her hot little feet over the dusty trail, her braids flying in the breeze.

When at last she reached the wagon, she fell exhausted into her mother's arms. Not a word could she say but, "Man! Man!"

"What is the matter, dear?" questioned Mrs. Phillips in an excited voice. "Tell me!" Sue could only sob and cry.

"Oh! An awful old man! He came right into the house," she wailed, "and began taking things."

When they reached the house, the robber had gone and had taken with him many of their valuables. Still, their loss did not seem very important to Mr. and Mrs. Phillips, since their little daughter was safe. That evening at family worship they all thanked God for His protection and loving care over Sue.

When she kissed her mother good night, Sue began to cry: "I won't ever stay alone again. I just can't do it," she sobbed.

"But, dear, you mustn't feel that way. Sometime it may be necessary. If you trust the Lord, He will take care of you just as He did today," assured her mother.

"I'll be brave, Mother," she promised as she crawled into bed.

However, Sue was no longer the same brave little girl she had been before. She was nervous, and would quiver and shake at the thought of being left alone.

"Wake up, wake up, Sue," Mrs. Phillips gently shook the bed one morning three weeks later. Sue slowly opened her big blue eyes. On her mother's face she saw a worried look.

"Sue," Mother began, "James Clark has just come on his horse to tell me that his mother is very ill. Father and Charles left for town about two hours ago, and they won't be home until after dark."

"But, Mother," began Sue in an anxious voice; then she shut her lips tightly and determined to do what her mother expected her to do.

"It seems I *must* go," Mrs. Phillips continued. "I knew that my little girl would understand."

Sue jumped out of bed and hit the floor with a thump. "I'll help you get ready," she exclaimed. Soon things were flying. Mrs. Phillips' cowhide satchel was packed, and she was ready to start. James had saddled a horse for her and was anxiously waiting.

Mrs. Phillips could plainly see fear written in her daughter's eyes. "Don't be afraid," she pleaded. Then—since tears were not too far away—"Take your embroidery work and go out to the hayloft if you are afraid to stay here at the house," she suggested. "I will probably be back before long. And remember, Sue, 'The angel of the Lord—'"

"Yes, I know, Mother," Sue put in; "I'll try to be brave."

As Sue saw her mother ride away, she was seized with terror. What if that awful man should come back? She became frantic. "Stop!" she screamed, but her mother was too far away to hear.

"I won't act this way," she resolved aloud, but her heart beat faster at the sound of her own voice. Hurriedly she gathered her embroidery work into a bundle and ran to the barn. When she got there, she could hardly climb the ladder to the loft, she was so frightened. She threw herself on the hay and tried to be calm, but she could only shake and tremble.

It seemed as if she had been there for hours, although it was only a few minutes, when she was suddenly impressed to go to the house. Something within her was saying, *Go to the house, Sue. Go to the house.*

That would be silly, she thought, *when I am afraid to stay here.* However, she felt that she *must* go; someone seemed to command her. She stood up shakily in the sweet-smelling hay and peered cautiously out of the small, dingy window.

All nature that met her eyes was calm and peaceful. The quaint little sod house and the large farmyard were bathed in the morning sunshine. Old Bossy stood below in the barnyard lazily chewing her cud. Sue could hear the drowsy hum of bees in the nearby hives. But within her heart there was no calmness.

Falteringly she descended the steps of the old ladder. She mechanically patted her great Maltese cat, which began purring and rubbing himself against her legs. She hurried to the house, calling the lively big ball of fur after her. He would keep her company.

As Sue came around the corner of the house, she suddenly stopped. There before her stood a man! He was smiling, and his handsome face seemed to be lit up with kindness. "Are you afraid, little girl?" he asked.

"Yes," she answered.

The kind stranger said, "Do not be afraid anymore."

A great calmness filled Sue's heart, and all her fears suddenly disappeared. Sue could not understand the change in her feelings. She looked back toward the barn, suddenly feeling shy. Then remembering her duty as hostess, she volunteered, "It certainly is a warm morning. May I get you a cold drink of water from the well?"

There was no answer. She turned to see why the man did not speak. No one was in sight. She walked slowly around the house, but saw only the great wide prairie stretching out in every direction. *Could it be*—she thought. Then softly she murmured, "'The angel of the Lord encampeth round about them that fear Him, and delivereth them.'"

Many years have passed since that memorable day, and Sue is now an old, gray-haired woman. But this experience has been a comfort to her many times through the years when she has needed the assurance that God and His angels are always near.

Man on a White Horse

JOHN JONES
AND W. A. SPICER

This particular story takes us back several centuries
to the early days of Methodism; the setting is northern Wales.

ᡩᡪᡡ

In the early days of Methodism, a minister of the Welsh Calvinistic Methodist Church, John Jones, of Flintshire, was traveling on horseback through a desolate region in northern Wales. According to his account, reprinted years ago in the London *Christian Herald*, he observed a rough-looking man, armed with a reaping hook, following him on the other side of a hedge, aiming to come up with him at a gate where it was necessary for the horseman to dismount.

The minister had a bag of money, which he had collected for a chapel building, and felt that not only the money, but possibly his life, was in danger. He stopped his horse and bowed his head to pray for special aid and protection. The horse was restive to go on, and on looking up after a moment of silent prayer, Jones saw a horseman on a white steed immediately alongside him. He was surprised and unable to account for the sudden and welcome appearance of a companion at such a moment. The story continues in his own words....

I described to the stranger the dangerous position in which I had been placed, and how relieved I felt by his sudden appearance. He made no reply; and on looking at his face, I saw that he was intently gazing in the direction of the gate. I followed his gaze, and saw the reaper emerge from his concealment, and run across a field to our left. He had evidently seen that I was no longer alone, and had given up his intended attempt.

All cause for alarm being now removed, I endeavored to enter into conversation with my deliverer, but again without the slightest success. Not a word did he give me in reply. I continued talking, however, as we rode toward the gate, though I utterly failed to see any reason for, and indeed felt rather hurt at, his silence. Only once did I hear his voice. Having watched the reaper disappear over the brow of a neighboring hill, I turned to my companion, and said, "Can it for a moment be doubted that my prayer was heard, and that you were sent for my deliverance by the Lord?" Then the horseman uttered the single word, "Amen." Not another word did he give, though I continued endeavoring to get from him replies to my questions, both in English and in Welsh.

We were now approaching the gate. I hurried on my horse for the purpose of opening it, and having done so, waited for him to pass through; he came not. I turned my head to seek for him—he was gone. I was dumbfounded. I looked back in the direction from which we had just been riding; he was not to be seen. He could not have gone through the gate, nor have made his horse leap the high hedges which on both sides shut in the road. Where was he? Could it be possible that I had seen no man or horse at all, and the vision was but a creature of my imagination? I tried hard to convince myself that this was the case, but in vain; for unless someone had been with me, why had the reaper, with his murderous-looking sickle, hurried away? No; this horseman was no creature of mine. Who could he have been?

I asked myself this question again and again, and then a feeling of profound awe began to creep over my soul. I remembered the singular manner in which he first appeared. I recollected his silence, and then again that single word to which he had given utterance had been elicited from him by mentioning the name of the Lord, and that this was the only occasion on which I had done so. What could I then believe? But one thing, and that was that my prayer had been heard, and that help had indeed been sent me at a time of peril. Full of this thought, I dismounted, and throwing myself on my knees at the side of the road, offered up a prayer of thankfulness to Him who had so signally preserved me from danger.

I then mounted my horse and continued on my journey. Through the years that have elapsed since that memorable July day, I have never for an instant wavered in the belief that I had a special providential deliverance.

The Trembling Terror

MARJORIE LEWIS LLOYD

Pastor John should have been dead, riddled with bullets.
Why wasn't he?

It happened in a country that I will not identify except to say that it is somewhere on this planet. And it happened to people who have never answered to the names used here. The important thing is that it happened!

The Terror. We might as well call him that. He was a bandit leader, a terrorist, and so ruthless a killer that the government had offered a huge reward for anyone who could bring him in, dead or alive.

Attempts to subdue him failed. He was out to destroy everything he didn't care for—and that included most everything and most everybody. This cunning bandit and his men were destroying everything in their path. The situation was desperate. People of his conquered territories needed medicine, food. But who would dare to enter the danger zone?

Finally a contingent of the government's finest soldiers went in. But the Terror quickly disposed of them with a simple trap. He had his men dig a huge pit and then place spears and sharpened iron stakes in the bottom of it. It was so carefully camouflaged that the soldiers marched right into it—to their death.

Then one day Pastor John received a call from a government official, asking if he would try to take some medicine into that area.

Pastor John and his little group of workers prayed earnestly about this assignment, this challenge, from the government. And as they prayed, they remembered the promise, "For he shall give his angels charge over thee, to keep thee in all thy ways. They shall bear thee up in their hands, lest thou dash thy foot against a stone" (Psalm 91:11-12).

They felt that they must try.

And so the government provided them with three or four aircraft loaded with food, clothing, and medicines. These supplies—about a hundred tons in all—were flown as near as possible to the area controlled by the Terror. Then a convoy of seventeen trucks and two or three jeeps was sent, ready to take the supplies into the stricken territory.

As Pastor John left on his dangerous mission, a government official said to him, "Be careful. But God is with you." He told Pastor John to work closely with his colonel in that section of the country.

But when Pastor John arrived, the colonel told him with a shake of his head, "It's impossible for you to go in." But then he said, "Wait. I have some soldiers that are on the fringes of that area, and at twelve o'clock each day they send me a report of the movements of the Terror."

It was on the fifth day that the report came in by radio that the Terror and his band had moved to another part of the country and that the main road into the area was now comparatively safe. They decided to go in the next morning.

The convoy was loaded from the warehouses, and Pastor John was given a government driver that he had used before—a young man by the name of Peter. Peter was a good Christian and a careful driver. Though his loyalty was to the government, he happened to be a member of the Terror's tribe, and so he knew the language. Pastor John, incidentally, had learned the Terror's tribal language too, as a young man, for he had worked in that area.

The group started out that morning, Pastor John and Peter in the lead jeep. The colonel had told them that the first part of their journey would be the most dangerous, as it wound through a valley. And as they drove through that valley, the pastor kept thinking of David's words, "the valley of the shadow of death." For it was just that. In the road were corpses that the Terror's men had left. Along the sides of the road were stakes, with women impaled on the stakes, gashed open—hideous scenes that one never expects to see in a lifetime.

Then, as they proceeded farther into the Terror's territory, the roads were so filled with dead bodies that the convoy was forced to stop. They tried to pull some of the bodies aside, but they could not, for it would delay them in reaching a point of safety that evening. So they just had to put those vehicles in four-wheel drive and grind over the corpses as they proceeded.

Eventually they got out of that valley. The colonel had told them that when they climbed the escarpment they would be out of the danger zone. And what a prayer of thanksgiving they offered when they reached the top!

They knew it would take the heavily loaded trucks about half an hour to get up that very difficult grade. So Peter and the pastor decided to go on and wait for them at a village a little way ahead.

They started on with lighter hearts. They could make better

time now over the high, level, flat plateau through clumps of dense jungle.

They were going through one of those dense clumps of jungle when suddenly Peter jerked the wheel to the left and they piled into the ditch, the jeep on its side. There they were, hugging each other tightly, and the pastor said, "What's your trouble? What happened?"

And Peter said, "Oh, we're going to die! They're going to kill us!"

"What's the matter?"

"Oh, I've seen the Terror's sign of an ambush! I've seen his sign!"

Only to his own tribesmen would the Terror give the warning. The secret sign was in a conspicuous place so that members of his own tribe would know that a trap lay ahead.

Two minutes passed. Three, four, maybe five minutes passed. Nothing happened. The pastor tried to climb out of the jeep, but Peter pulled him back on top of him again. "No! You must not get out!"

Finally, with great difficulty, Pastor John *did* climb out. He stood at the edge of the road and looked around. He could see nothing suspicious—except that there were fresh tracks in the road. And he had the strange feeling that he was being watched.

He was impressed by the Spirit of God to say something. So he put his portable loud speaker to his mouth and spoke in the language of the tribe through whose territory they were passing. He just said to the trees and the jungle around him, "We have come as friends. I am a Christian pastor. I am here to help you. Anybody in this area who needs help, we are here to help you. We are not here as enemies but as friends."

Nothing happened. Everything was quiet. It was deathly still!

Then out of the silence came the snap of two dry twigs. Snap! Snap! It was a signal—a signal that Pastor John had learned as a boy. It was a challenging signal, and a reply must be given. Someone off in the jungle was challenging their passage. If he could come up with the right word, everything would be all right. But it had been twelve or fourteen years since he had used that word— that password—and he had forgotten it.

He flashed a message on the frequency of heaven. And like another flash, that word came back to the tip of his tongue. He shouted it out. It was the right word!

Again he said through his loudspeaker, "Friend, whoever you are out there, please come and let's shake hands." And he gave in the tribal language the respectful greeting that only the big chiefs receive. Again nothing happened.

Then, off to the right, there was a rustle in the jungle. The leaves moved, and onto the edge of the road stepped a tall, hand-some, fine-looking warrior with an automatic rifle in his hand, pointed right at him.

The pastor said, "Friend, put down your gun, please. I have no weapons. I'm here as a friend."

The warrior took two or three more steps toward him, with that automatic rifle still pointed right at him. Pastor John could see that the man was some high ranking leader. Again he gave the respectful greeting.

Finally the warrior laid down his gun and approached cau-tiously, suspiciously. As he approached, the pastor extended his hand. The warrior looked at him, clasped his hand, and said in sur-prise, "Pastor John, what are you doing here?"

He had war paint on his forehead and cheeks. The pastor couldn't recognize him, and so he said, "Do you know me?"

"Yes, yes, of course I know you. Don't you know me?"

"Who are you?"

"I am the Terror."

The pastor was holding a huge reward in his hand, as it were. And this terribly feared bandit knew him!

"Don't you remember? I am Henry from the village of Wait. You used to teach us in your little Sabbath School, thirteen or fifteen years ago. I am Henry. Don't you remember me, Pastor John?"

Of course he remembered him! And the boy Henry was now this feared bandit!

As the pastor held his hand, the Terror began to tremble like a leaf in the wind. His whole body was shaking. He said, "Now I understand. Now I understand. For the first time in my life my voice disappeared. My voice was taken from me. I tried to give an order as your jeep went into the ditch—an order for my men to kill. But I couldn't find a voice. My voice was taken away. And as I looked at the wheels spinning around on your jeep, I could see soldiers standing around, heavily armed. I could see these soldiers off in the road behind you. They didn't look like any soldiers I have ever seen."

He went on. "Now I understand. Those stories you used to tell us, those picture rolls you used to show us—of your God, of those angels that your God sends." He was still trembling. "Now I understand. Those beings that looked like the moon and like the stars were angels from your God! Oh, Pastor John, what are you doing here?"

What a thrill! He told the Terror what he was doing there. And he knew that those mighty angels from heaven were still standing right there beside them. For this terrible killer, this man skilled in destruction and death, was still trembling!

They talked for two or three minutes, and then the Terror

heard the trucks approaching. He said, "Pastor John, are there soldiers in those trucks?"

"Yes, Henry, but they are under my control. They are under my orders."

"Oh, but they will kill me!"

He had heard. He knew that there was a tremendous price on his head. But the pastor assured him, "There will be no killing here today. God and His angels are here. There will be no killing today!"

The trucks were still some distance away, and the pastor said to him, "Friend, you have seen today a wonderful demonstration of God's love for you. I did not see those soldiers, those angels that you saw. But I know that just one of those angels could have annihilated you and your men. But God loves you. That same Jesus that you heard about under the trees in the village of Wait, fifteen years ago, is still speaking to you. Promise me, friend—promise me, Henry—that you will give up this life of destruction, that you will respect and honor the love of the Jesus who has saved your life, who wants to give you eternal life with Him!"

Still trembling, the Terror hesitated and looked around. The pastor asked how many men he had with him in the jungle and asked him to call them. He gave an order, and dozens of heavily armed bandits came out from both sides of that jungle. They couldn't understand what had happened to their proud and haughty leader who grasped the hand of a white man, a member of the race they were sworn to destroy. They looked at him with cruelty and death in their eyes.

As his men approached, the Terror said to them, "This man's skin is white, but his heart is the same as ours. He is our friend."

They gathered around him, and he told them about his voice disappearing, about the soldiers from heaven, and that the pastor had assured him they were still standing there, watching over their meeting.

Then the pastor asked him again, "Will you promise to give up this terrible life of destruction and slaughter?"

And there in the presence of his men—he promised!

It took a long time to persuade the government that the Terror was a converted man. Top officials were convinced only when they saw that the horrible reign of terror had completely subsided. Then another proclamation was issued, explaining briefly that the Terror was now a Christian and that the price on his head was no longer an offer. The radio blared the news. The newspapers carried it in headlines.

And Pastor John remembered the words of his father, spoken to him as a frightened boy of ten, "Son, our Father in heaven has sent His angels to be with us. Everything will be all right."

Now You See Them

RUTH WHEELER

He stopped at the house to borrow a light.
Little did he know what would come with that light.

Pastor Merritt Warren had not been in China long when he made this particular trip. Like most every journey he would take in that country, it was full of danger, leading through a robber-infested area.

He had been traveling several days when he was delayed one afternoon by a stranger who invited him to his home. The person had learned that Pastor Warren was a Christian minister and wanted to ask questions about his beliefs. Pastor Warren, of course, was glad for the opportunity to talk with one who showed such interest.

He thought he had plenty of time. The coolies, with the boxes, had gone on. The village of Chintaipu was only five miles away. He could easily ride that distance before dark. As he was leaving, however, his host told him that it was nearly three times that far. He warned him that it was not safe to travel in that region after dark.

Hastily Pastor Warren mounted his horse and hurried over the low hills. Just at dark he reached a small village along the way. He hoped the carriers would be waiting there. But he learned that they had gone on up the mountain.

What could he do? The carriers had his food and his bedding. And he must pay for their lodging wherever they stopped. He knew now that he was in danger.

The coolies had his lantern, too, and he would have to have a lantern. So he bought a Chinese paper lantern, and the shopkeeper lighted it for him.

But in a little while, as he walked ahead, leading his horse down the slippery stones of the mountain, the candle sputtered and went out. He started to light another, but then he said to himself, *Now, look here! You can see better with the lantern, but so can the robbers. If they are following you, the light will help them more than it will help you.* So he trudged on, hoping the robbers wouldn't hear the clank of the horse's shoes on the stone steps.

At the bottom of the mountain he came to a bridge made of stone slabs. Pastor Warren couldn't see what he was crossing—it might be a stream or a chasm. He could see only the dim trail and the bridge. Beyond the bridge the trail turned to the right and began another ascent.

About a hundred and fifty feet from the bridge, to his right, Pastor Warren saw a house and a light burning inside. The house was about fifty feet long and seemed to face the road. A door in the center opened as he arrived, and two men came out.

Pastor Warren had a good excuse for stopping, for he was alone and without a light. Speaking in the humble manner used by the Chinese, he said politely, "May your younger brother borrow a light from his older brother?"

"I shall be glad to give my brother a light," one of the men answered. He stepped inside and returned with a piece of flaming bamboo. When the candle in the lantern had been lighted, one of the men asked, "Where are you going?"

"To Chintaipu."

"I am traveling that way myself."

"I shall be honored to have my older brother lead me," Pastor Warren answered.

They started off together, talking as they traveled. The pastor asked questions, but he was careful not to say anything that would sound as if he were trying to identify his companion. If the man were a robber, the situation would be dangerous.

Finally the man said, "There are many robbers through this section, and they are robbing all the time. No one is really safe on this road. I am glad I could come along with you."

That was strange. The man wore ordinary clothes, the rice-straw sandals of the common peasant. Why would anyone try to rob him? And why was this stranger happy to have a foreigner with him?

Soon they came to a place where a path branched off. The Chinese man said, "I must leave you here."

"Aren't you going to Chintaipu?"

"No, I'm turning off here."

"How much farther is it to Chintaipu?"

"Not very far. You will be there right away. I am glad I could walk with you."

When Pastor Warren arrived in the village, he found the people worried about his safety. They told of many travelers who had been robbed, some even killed. The young missionary had reason to be thankful—very, very thankful!

The next time he traveled that way, he was anxious to see by daylight the places where he had walked that dark night. It was all just as he remembered it. The shop where he had bought the lantern. The climb up the mountain. The stone steps down the other side. The ravine with the stone slabs for crossing. As he started up the slope, he looked for the house.

No house was there!

Had the house burned down? "It has to be here!" he exclaimed. "It was a large house, and it stood right here!" But as he examined that slope, he saw that the ground had never been leveled at any place along the road. It would have been impossible to build a house without leveling a large piece of ground. But there was no level ground. The hillside had never been disturbed!

No wonder he stood silently with bowed head. He knew now that an angel had walked with him that dark night!

When the Fire Went Out

LOUISE DUBAY AND C. F. O'DELL

The Far North wields a terrible icy sword. Without blessed warmth,
life cannot survive more than minutes when the thermometer
leaves zero behind and plummets into numbing cold.

❧

It happened in a little cabin in Anchorage, Alaska, on a cold February morning. Mrs. Louise Dubay was alone and so badly crippled that she could not walk without applying hot-and-cold treatments to her leg. The cabin was heated by a wood-burning cookstove. She had many friends, but this morning for some reason no one had remembered to visit her and bring in a fresh supply of wood. And she couldn't call anyone, because she had no telephone at that time. In her desperation she began to pray aloud. Never before had she prayed so earnestly. But no one came.

Finally the last of the wood was gone, and the fire went out. It was thirty degrees below zero. The cabin began to chill rapidly, and she knew that, even protected as she was by blankets, she would soon freeze to death unless someone came and brought in wood for her. She kept praying, but no one came. And then she prayed a different kind of prayer. She told the Lord that if it was His will that she freeze to death, it was all right. She was willing.

About that time the door opened—the cabin had only one

door—and in walked a tall young man carrying an armload of wood. He was not dressed as most people dress in Alaska during the winter months. He had on a black hat and a black overcoat. He put the wood in the woodbox and proceeded to make a fire in the stove. When the fire was burning well, he put water in the big teakettle and placed it over the fire.

All this time he seemed to keep his face turned so that she could not see his full face. He turned now and went out the door, returning shortly with another armload of firewood. She still had not really seen his face. Nor had he said a word.

Naturally Mrs. Dubay was awed by all this—so much so that she could not speak. She just sat there and looked at him, all the while wanting to ask him if he was an angel, yet afraid to speak up. Finally she asked him that question in her mind, without saying a word aloud. And when she did that, he turned toward her, smiled, and nodded his head. His face was so noble, she says, that she knew he was not from this world. He turned, opened the door, and left without saying a word.

For a time she just sat there, as if petrified. Finally she thought, *If he is an angel sent from God, there will not be any footprints in the snow outside the door.* So she forced herself to hobble to the door, opened it, and looked out on the unruffled snow. There were no footprints. Neither had the snow been disturbed over or around her little pile of wood. The snow was perfectly smooth and rounded over as always after a snowstorm!

Angels Unawares

WANDA CHILSON

Sixteen-year-old Ted was plainly worried. That stranger on horseback had asked far too many questions. With Mother and Father gone, what could they do should the stranger return during the night?

Marlene sat in a comfortable chair near the fireplace. In her lap lay an open Bible. Her face wore a puzzled expression. The text she had just finished reading—what did it mean?

Uncle Jim who sat close by laughed merrily. "Marlene, you look as if you were about to take castor oil."

"Oh, I was trying to think, Uncle Jim. You know this verse in Hebrews 13:2. It goes, 'Be not forgetful to entertain strangers: for thereby some have entertained angels unawares.' Did anyone really ever entertain an angel when he didn't know it?"

"Oh, yes, Marlene. You remember the angels that visited Abraham and Lot, and then there was—"

"Yes, but I mean *now*," interrupted Marlene. "Things like that don't happen anymore do they? I *wish* they would."

"Well, now, I'm not so sure they don't. Come over here and sit on the arm of my chair. I'm going to tell you a story."

The little girl climbed joyously upon the arm of the chair and laid her soft golden curls on her big uncle's shoulder.

"I haven't told many people this story, Marlene," said Uncle Jim. "It seems almost too wonderful an experience to talk about. But I believe it will help you and answer your question."

When I was a very small boy, our family lived in a large log house in the Rocky Mountains. It was early winter, before any hard storms had come, and Mother and Father had been called away to attend a friend's funeral. Before they left they made provision for us children. Father brought plenty of wood, and Mother cooked a whole day to be sure we would have plenty while she was away. We were all alone—big brother Ted, baby sister, and I—but we were not afraid. The valley where we lived was seldom visited by anyone. We were there only because Father's government work required it.

We played and worked all day long. The hill south of our house provided fine sliding and skiing. While we were sliding in the late afternoon, a man on horseback rode up and began to ask questions. Brother Ted motioned for me to be still, and answered as well as he could. The stranger wanted to know all about our family, where Father and Mother were, and when they would be home. Finally he rode away, and we finished our sliding. But Ted was not so jolly after that. However, because I thought Ted, who was sixteen years old, was not afraid of anything, I soon forgot all about the strange man. I learned later that he felt uneasy about a sum of money belonging to the United States government, which Father had hidden under the floor by our cellar door.

Quite suddenly a severe storm broke. Ted and I hastened to get the chores done. After supper we went to the living room, where the fire burned warm and bright. Ted told Bible stories for a while, and then we knelt and asked our heavenly Father to watch over us and care for our parents so far away.

Then Ted brought apples, we popped corn, and before long we were having loads of fun. Ted was playing horseback for our little sister, when a knock came at the door. It surprised us. Big brother looked at me for a long while. The knock came again more loudly than before. Ted walked to the door and opened it. A tired and apparently half-starved man staggered in. Ted helped him remove his heavy boots and coat, and had him sit before the roaring fire. He did not speak for a while, but when he did, I felt as if I had always known him. Little sister walked over to him, and after looking at him intently, climbed into his lap.

We got some hot food for him to eat. Afterward Ted told him where he was to sleep, and we all went to bed.

In the middle of the night Ted awoke with a start; someone was rattling the door; it opened, and the person walked in. Ted, thinking it was the stranger, felt at ease. But after some moments, a different noise started, and he decided to investigate.

Cautiously peering from the bedroom door, he saw a light and a figure over by the cellar door. He was somewhat frightened and a little angry. He called out to the man to leave. But the thief only laughed and stood up. He walked toward Ted, who immediately recognized him as the stranger who had asked so many questions. Suddenly, just as he was about to strike Ted, a bright light appeared in the doorway of the room where the stranger of the storm was supposed to be asleep, and a voice said, "Go, thief!"

The intruder dropped his weapon in surprise, backed toward the outside door, and still not taking his eyes from the light, slipped out into the darkness. The latch clicked, and he was gone.

The moment the door clicked, the light disappeared. The young stranger spoke to Ted from the next room. They stood together, listening to the pound of the horse's hoofs, as the would-be robber rode away. Then they went to bed again, and strange to say, Ted fell asleep immediately.

When the first rosy morning light shone through the bedroom windows, we were up. But the stranger was already out getting wood for the fire. Brother Ted was a fine cook, and breakfast was soon ready. Much to our surprise, the stranger said grace when we bowed our heads. After breakfast, he decided to hurry on, for his journey should not be delayed, he said.

He thanked us graciously and started over the newly fallen snow, up the hill behind our house. After waiting some time for him to reappear on the top of the hill, Ted became alarmed and determined to go see what had happened to him.

A few moments after he left, I found a white card on the bed where the stranger had slept.

Two hours later Ted came home. He said he could find no trace of the man, and that just behind the house the tracks had stopped. Brother seemed greatly mystified and uneasy about the whole thing, until I gave him the little white card. After reading it, he found a chair, taking baby sister in his lap, he read aloud, as I stood at his arm, "Be not forgetful to entertain strangers: for thereby some have entertained angels unawares."

Ted took my hand in his and said, "Jimmy Boy, you may not understand, but I know that man was an angel sent to protect us."

Uncle Jim sat for a moment in silence. Then Marlene slid into his lap, looked into his kind eyes and exclaimed, "Now I truly understand. Angels are with us right now, every day, and if we do as we should and serve our heavenly Father, they will keep us from harm."

"Yes," smiled Uncle Jim, "and you may even see one someday, and not realize that you have seen an angel."

Angels on Guard

VON ASSELT

"For often an inexplicable, unutterable fear would come over us, so that we had to get up at night, and go on our knees to pray...."

The following story of deliverance is preserved in the records of missionary pioneering in the Dutch East Indies, the populous islands that gave Holland a dominion in the Orient. The incident occurred in the life of Von Asselt, a Rhenish missionary in Sumatra from 1856 to 1876, and was related by him when on a visit to Lübeck. The account was subsequently reproduced in the Sontagsblatt für's Hans.

When I first was sent to Sumatra, in the year 1856, I was the first European missionary to go among the wild Battaks, although twenty years prior two American missionaries had come to them with the gospel, but they had been killed and eaten. Since then no effort had been made to bring the gospel to these people, and naturally they had remained the same cruel savages.

What it means for one to stand alone among a savage people, unable to make himself understood, not understanding a single sound of their language, but whose suspicious, hostile looks and gestures speak only a too-well-understood language—yes, it is hard for one to comprehend that. The first two years that I spent among the Battaks, at first all alone and then afterward with my wife, were so hard that it makes me shudder even now when I think of them. Often it seemed as if we were not only encompassed by hostile men, but also by hostile powers of darkness; for often an inexplicable, unutterable fear would come over us, so that we had to get up at night, and go on our knees to pray or read the Word of God, in order to find relief.

After we had lived in this place for two years, we moved several hours' journey inland, among a tribe somewhat civilized, who received us more kindly. There we built a small house with three rooms—a living room, a bedroom, and a small reception room—and life for us became a little more easy and cheerful.

When I had been in this new place for some months, a man came to me from the district where we had been, and whom I had known there. I was sitting on the bench in front of our house, and he sat down beside me, and for a while talked of this, that, and the other. Finally he began: "Now, *tuan* [teacher], I have yet one request."

"And what is that?"

"I would like to have a look at your watchmen close at hand."

"What watchmen do you mean? I do not have any," I replied.

"I mean the watchmen whom you station around your house at night, to protect you."

"But I have no watchmen," I said again. "I have only a little herd boy and a little cook, and they would make poor watchmen."

Then the man looked at me incredulously, as if he wished to say, "Oh, do not try to make me believe otherwise, for I know better."

Then he asked: "May I look through your house, to see if they are hid there?"

"Yes, certainly," I said, laughing. "Look through it; you will not find anybody." So he went in and searched in every corner, even through the beds, but came to me very much disappointed.

"Then I began a little probing myself and requested him to tell me the circumstances about those watchmen of whom he spoke, and this is what he related to me:

"When you first came to us, *tuan*, we were very angry at you. We did not want you to live among us. We did not trust you and believed you had some design against us. Therefore we came together and resolved to kill you and your wife. Accordingly, we went to your house night after night, but when we came near, there stood always, close around the house, a double row of watchmen with glittering weapons, and we did not venture to attack them to get into your house. But we were not willing to abandon our plan, so we went to a professional assassin [there still was among the savage Battaks at that time a special guild of assassins, who killed for hire anyone whom the tribe desired to get out of the way], and asked him if he would undertake to kill you and your wife. He laughed at us because of our cowardice, and said, 'I fear no God and no devil. I will get through those watchmen easily.' So we came all together in the evening, and the assassin, swinging his weapon about his head, went courageously on before us. As we neared your house, we remained behind and let him go on alone. But in a short time he came running back hastily, and said, 'No, I dare not risk it to go through alone; two rows of big, strong men stand there, very close together, shoulder to shoulder, and their weapons shine like fire.' Then we gave it up to kill you. But, now, tell me, *tuan*, who are those watchmen? Have you never seen them?"

"No, I have never seen them," I said.

"'And your wife did not see them?'

"No, my wife did not see them."

"But yet we have all seen them; how is that?" he asked.

Then I went in and brought a Bible from our house, and holding it open before him, said, "See here; this book is the Word of our great God, in which He promises to guard and defend us, and we firmly believe that Word; therefore we need not see the watchmen. But you do not believe, therefore the great God has to show you the watchmen, in order that you may learn to believe."

Five

WE SHALL CALL UPON HIM, AND HE WILL ANSWER

Ask, and it shall be given you; seek, and ye shall find;
knock, and it shall be opened unto you: For every one
that asketh receiveth; and he that seeketh findeth;
and to him that knocketh it shall be opened.

MATTHEW 7:7-8

May Sheridan Gold, in her story in this section, dared to take God at His word, praying Matthew 7:7-8 every hour during the longest night of her life. The other stories in this section tell of others who took certain Scriptural promises to the bank. Clearly, God and His angels take most seriously prayer requests that are guaranteed by God's Holy Book in the same way that bank depositors all across America deposit their lifetime savings without a worry in the world, knowing that those deposits are guaranteed by the Federal Reserve System.

But banking on God's promises without a willingness to follow through, to show Him your sincerity and commitment by single-minded and single-focused vigil, is not likely to be as successful as May Sheridan Gold's laying siege to her Lord's promise:

I know it was not just the novena that brought healing. It was prayer, repeated prayer, ceaseless prayer, unrelenting prayer—our own, plus the prayers of others—that brought us to the point where we relinquished the problem to God.

But note that the banking on God's promises was but the first step; relinquishment was the all-important second.

The Nine-Hour Prayer

MAY SHERIDAN GOLD

Andy's eye was badly hurt—so badly that doctors gave him the slimmest of chances that he would ever see again. Slim though they were, his mother decided to pray the Nine-Hour Novena every hour.

He was only six years old when the accident happened. I don't know how I knew it was really serious, for he complained of no pain, but I knew—I was positive.

Andy had been out in the front yard helping his dad get rid of some tall weeds in the vacant lot adjoining our property. Suddenly he came in the front door wiping moisture from his left cheek and said, "My eye is watering, Mommy."

I'll never know how or why I was so certain, but I felt a reaction like a blow in the pit of my stomach, and words formed in my mind, *His eye is hurt badly.* After trying to say some calming words to him, I went straight to the phone to call the pediatrician. It was 11:30 A.M. on a sunny Saturday. I told Doctor Wiedman that Andy's eye was hurt and that I needed for him to see Andy right away.

My husband Dan came in, and was surprised to find me calling the doctor since Andy was not even crying or saying that his eye hurt. But perhaps he thought my anxiety was due to the fact that I was expecting a baby, our third child, in two months.

While driving the two miles to Doctor Wiedman's, I looked over at Andy, and with a sense of shock noted that his left eye was no longer shiny and blue. It looked dull, gray, and almost flat. When we stopped at a light, I asked him to cover his right eye with his hand and tell me if he could see me. "No! That's funny," he said, "I can't see."

When we entered Doctor Wiedman's office, he greeted us, and after one hard look at Andy across the room, he left to bring back the eye specialist near his office. The eye doctor was very kind, but after a quick look and a few questions, he left. He returned quickly to say, "Mrs. Gold, there is one eye surgeon in this town who I feel might be able to help. I've called him at the Episcopal Eye, Ear, Nose, and Throat Hospital, and he will meet you there." Noting my condition, both doctors suggested that my husband come and drive us there, which he did.

When the three of us reached the hospital, Dr. John Harry King greeted us in the gentlest way. He examined Andy deftly, talking to him reassuringly as he did so. He spoke to us privately. "Mr. and Mrs. Gold, the cornea of Andy's eye has somehow been pierced, perhaps by a thorn. The reason it looks dull is that all of the fluid has gone out through the hole. Unfortunately there is no surgery that we can perform."

"Is there any chance the eye can be saved?" I asked, desperately.

He paused, carefully choosing his words. "Yes, Mrs. Gold, a faint chance. The hole could heal and some of the fluid could re-form. But, I must warn you it is a very, very slim chance—a medical rarity." He agreed that we should give the eye every chance for any possible healing, and as this meant both eyes must be bandaged, we felt I should stay with Andy in the hospital.

It was a very old hospital, and they led us to a long, narrow room where they put Andy in a bed with sides to be sure he didn't fall. A cot was brought in for me, and our vigil of keeping a healthy, active, six-year-old boy with bandaged eyes completely still and quiet began. When I quickly went home for a suitcase and some books to read to him, I made several calls, asking for prayers for our Andy.

Back at the hospital, the long evening finally drew to a close, and as things quieted down, I hoped Andy would sleep. Before he did, I asked him to pray with me. I'd found a special prayer at home, one I'd had but never used, except to read it casually. It was called a Nine-Hour Novena, and I had always liked its wording. "Ask and ye shall receive; seek and ye shall find; knock and it shall be opened to you. Dear Lord, I ask, I seek, I knock, and request that my petition be granted."

Andy repeated each phrase after me. I intended to make the prayer for him at hourly intervals all night long. He asked me to wake him so he could pray too.

Though there was no air conditioning and the room was stifling hot, Andy quickly fell asleep. When I was sure he wouldn't hear me, I knelt beside the cot and wept. But then, prayer came, "Dear Lord, please heal Andy's eye…he wasn't doing anything wrong or being silly…he was helping his dad. You know how he always notices everything in the house with his bright eyes, how he can find things for us all, how he tries to help watch his little brother. Oh, please, please don't let that eye be blinded." Then I added a special request, "Help me to wake each hour, on the hour, to say the novena." As tired as I was, this was asking a great deal.

I seemed to fall asleep quickly, as Andy had. I woke up later and looked at my watch. It was exactly 11 p.m. I knelt again, and read the prayer from a light in the hall. I whispered, "Andy?" He, too, was awake and joined me in the prayer, then seemed to go right back to sleep. I drowsed off too, but at midnight some inner alarm clock sounded and I prayed again. After the third time this happened, exactly this way, I was no longer surprised. It seemed natural and right and I somehow felt sure it was God's way of letting us know we were in His care.

When I read the prayer for the sixth time—at 3 A.M.—I felt the greatest warmth and sense of comfort I can recall. The words came alive, bringing tears of gratitude to my eyes. Though I didn't hear an audible voice inside, I felt God speaking to me, reassuring me, inviting me to let go, to relinquish Andy's problem to Him.

"Thank You, Lord," I murmured, "for caring, for staying so close at this time. Yes, I trust You to deal with Andy's eye." I had no way of knowing if my child would indeed see again, but whatever happened, I knew God would help us through the ordeal. I felt so very loved, somehow, in that dismal little room.

At 6 A.M., as we said the prayer for the last time, we heard activities beginning in the hallways. Doctor King had agreed to come in early—around 8:30 I think—and my husband and I met him when he arrived. The doctor talked with Andy a bit before beginning to remove the bandage to check for possible infection.

As he took the bandage off, I saw the incredulous look on Doctor King's face. Then I looked at Andy.

The eye was round again! It was bright blue and shining, exactly like the other eye.

"Mrs. Gold, what have you done?" the doctor exclaimed. It was, in retrospect, an odd question. When I told him quickly and briefly of our nine-hour prayer, the doctor himself had tears in his eyes. Gently he covered Andy's "good" eye, held up two fingers and asked, "How many?" Andy said, "Two," then replied correctly to other tests Doctor King tried.

"This is most gratifying," Doctor King said. "I've never seen anything like it."

Along with our joy and gratitude, he had to caution us, however. Now proper care was more important than ever. Andy must not risk bumping his head, which might collapse his eye. He must remain still, with both eyes bandaged. Infection could occur, so he must take antibiotics. A few days later, Doctor King soberly told me that I must realize that though his eye might be saved cosmetically, I must not expect his vision to be normal. But, whenever I prayed, I seemed to remember that the whole thing had been handed over to God, and surely that must include Andy's vision.

Our next weeks were difficult ones, with five more days in the hospital and strict bed care at home to follow. Our second son, Skip, had to be sent to his grandparents to help keep things calm for Andy. We visited Doctor King's office every third day, which meant a trip all the way to town, with Andy, by then, wearing a patch over one eye. When the day finally came to conduct a vision test, we discovered, joyfully, that the vision in that eye was almost normal, and in later years it became perfect. The last time Doctor King saw Andy, he could not even find the scar where the hole was until he consulted his chart, because it had become so tiny.

Looking back, I know it was not just the novena that brought healing. It was prayer, repeated prayer, ceaseless prayer, unrelenting prayer—our own, plus the prayers of others—that brought us to the point where we relinquished the problem to God. To this day, if you ask him, Doctor King, the very famous eye surgeon whose cornea-preservation technique led to the beginning of the International Eye Foundation, will tell you that it was prayer that brought about one of the most remarkable occurrences he has ever witnessed—the restoration of a small boy's eye.

The Shetland Pony

V. F. SMITH

He said to his host, "It seems it's not what you pray for,
but who does the praying!"

Three little girls, and three little girls who were visiting them, suddenly decided they wanted to get the Shetland pony and take turns riding.

There was no reason they shouldn't ride, except that the pony was out in the south pasture, running with some yearling steers. And this particular pony loved her freedom. She could run faster than most Shetlands, and she knew every trick of escape. It took two well-mounted men to bring her in.

The father who owned the horse explained to the girls that he couldn't bring her in alone, and he tried to suggest something else they might do. But after a hurried conference the six little girls just dropped to their knees and began to pray. The problem, to them, was so simple. God could bring the pony in.

It was a sight to remember—six little girls with their heads together, praying so earnestly. The father was almost moved to join them. But he wondered if it might not be a sacrilege to pray for a range-running horse to come home. And it seemed so futile.

He was about to tell them that one doesn't ask God for such things, when he looked up and saw the pony coming on the run—down the butte, across the flat, through the creek, and into the corral, where she stopped and waited. The girls by now were up from their knees and waiting for her. They weren't even surprised. They just ran for her with cries of joy, got her bridled, and took her off for an afternoon of riding.

The father of the visiting girls was absolutely shaken. His face was white. He said to his host, "It seems it's not what you pray for, but who does the praying!"

He had just seen six little girls blast every known principle of horse behavior. He wouldn't have believed the story if it had been told him. But he had seen it and couldn't forget. He began reading his Bible and then attending church with his family. He has since held several offices in the church. Before witnessing what happened that day, religion had meant nothing to him. His faith is now unshakable!

He Shall Keep Thee

LUCILLE TAYLOR

*The Civil War, deadliest of all American wars, was raging.
So many men had died that new recruits were desperately needed
to fill their places. If they failed to volunteer, they were conscripted
by force—not just men, but boys, too.*

❧

"Ding," and then "ticktock, ticktock, ticktock." Once more the old clock above the kitchen cabinet announced to the busy farm wife that the noon hour had arrived.

Hastily opening the oven door, she brought out two luscious apple pies and set them on the windowsill to cool.

"Janet, run to the springhouse and get that fresh pan of cream. You may whip it for the pies. Hurry, for I must send Teddy for Tom and Larry soon. The poor boys must be getting hungry." Mother Dawson filled a dish with steaming baked sweet potatoes.

Tom and Larry had been plowing since early morning, and as the sun approached the zenith, their appetites were increasing to capacity. When little Teddy called them to dinner, they fed the horses and started toward the house.

Larry was an average boy of fourteen, with freckled face and unruly blond hair; his brother, who was two years his senior, was tall, slim, and shy.

Father Dawson had been compelled to leave his family a month before when a group of soldiers forced all the men in the countryside to go to the battlefield. For it was 1862 and the Civil War, or "the War Between the States," was raging in North America. Mrs. Dawson had managed things quite well. She was a woman of steady nerve and common sense combined with undaunted courage. Her trust was in God, and she knew that He had not forgotten her family. Tom and Larry took over the farm work, and they showed themselves to be quite equal to the task. Twelve-year-old Janet was Mother's dependable helper at whatever duty was assigned her. Three younger children—Teddy, five, and the twins, three—added to the responsibility.

As the boys neared the house, pleasant odors met them, and their quick strides broke into a run.

The five of them were soon seated around the well-spread table. The twins, who had not awakened from their morning nap, were left to sleep.

Since Mr. Dawson had been gone, the family had spent much time in prayer. Never did they pray but that they earnestly entreated God for His protection for Father, and also that they would be saved from danger. It was Mrs. Dawson who asked Heaven's blessing on this meal, and then finished: "Loving Father, we know that Thou seest us and knowest our condition. We know that Thou knowest where Father is, and we ask that Thou wilt care for him. Help us to do our work as Thou wouldst do it. Don't let anything happen to any of us unless it is Thy will. We trust in Thee. Amen."

In a crude army camp similar prayers ascended heavenward. Father Dawson's mind was continually on his family at home. He realized the perils that they might have to meet, and he longed to help them; however, he had no means of communication, and he could only trust in God. Fervent and sincere were the prayers that came from his agonizing heart. He firmly believed that God would grant his petition and make it possible for him to return to his family. But how? And when?

For a while, the little group around the dinner table ate in silence. They were thankful that a loving heavenly Father so bountifully supplied their needs, for they lacked nothing. But only yesterday they had heard rumors that a band of soldiers was coming through that section of the state. Although they still believed that God would protect them, they felt a certain uneasiness. Often, as Mrs. Dawson went about her duties, she would glance down the long, dusty road as if visualizing a dust cloud in the distance. But her confidence was in God, and not once did she allow herself to appear fearful before her children.

Larry told of his adventure in catching a calf that had broken away. Tom answered his mother's questions about the cotton over behind the hill. Teddy contributed to the conversation a vivid word picture of the mud dam, which had been his project of the morning. Janet was in a thoughtful mood, and her eyes wore a dreamy expression as her glance wandered aimlessly out the window and down the dusty road. Suddenly her face turned pale.

"Look!" she exclaimed, bending over the table with eyes fixed far down the highway. Four other pairs of eyes followed Janet's. There was a dust cloud in the distance, advancing fast and coming closer.

"I do believe—" began Mother after a breathless instant, and then she realized the terrible truth. The same men were coming who had taken her husband. With a gasp she jumped from her seat.

"Boys, hide. Go outside. Quick!"

Instantly the boys ran from the house and down into the corn-field. Silently they lay down behind the highest stalks.

The men were almost to the house.

"The twins, mother—" and before finishing, Janet dashed off toward the sleeping youngsters.

"Yes, get them," and Mother herself hastened to bring one of the children from the bed.

The frightened youngsters, half asleep, were set in the places left vacant by the older boys, and admonished, "Eat." They looked rather puzzled at the half-eaten food, but having been taught to obey, they ate without asking any questions. Mother and Janet sat down in their places and tried to look calm. The two soldiers drove their horses into the yard and jumped from the saddles. Without a word of explanation they bolted into the house.

"Have you any men?" one of them demanded, while the other stalked through the house, looking under beds and behind doors.

"Sir, we are eating dinner. You see there are no men here," answered Mrs. Dawson with a gesture toward the circle around the table. "You have taken my husband. What more do you want?" Though pale, she remained calm. Janet tried to appear uncon-cerned. The three younger children, stiff with fright, only stared at the intruders, who after a few terrible moments, assured themselves that no men were in the house, and without a word went into the backyard. One of them ran out to the cornfield and looked down the rows, but seeing no one, he ran back to his comrade, who was already impatiently climbing into his saddle. Two shots were fired into the air, and the men were off.

Two sober-eyed boys standing in the cornfield watched the dis-appearing dust cloud that veiled the two gray-clad riders. Then, without a word they walked back to the house.

A bewildered yet happy little family stood in silence by the kitchen window, and stared down the long, dusty road.

It was Mother Dawson who broke the silence. As she quoted the precious promise in her quiet voice, it seemed as if an angel spoke: " 'For he shall give his angels charge over thee, to keep thee in all thy ways.' Children, God *has* kept His promise; He always does, and He will take care of Father, too."

In humble gratitude the little group bowed to praise God for their deliverance. Prayer was not foreign to this family; each child had prayed at the family altar since babyhood.

As they arose, a man could be seen approaching. It was little Teddy whose sharp eyes first detected the traveler.

"Mother, a man is coming," he announced. "He is walking." Once more the family gathered by the window, wondering who the man might be. As he came closer, there seemed to be something strangely familiar in his walk. The little group watched intently. They rarely had visitors.

"It's Father!" exclaimed Larry, running out of the house. The others followed him joyously. The man hastened his steps, and only God knows the happiness that leaped into the hearts of those present at that family reunion.

Prayer in Shorthand

Minnie Waite Brown

*It was just a prayer written in shorthand. Not being able to read
shorthand, he put it in the back of his typing book
and forgot about it—for twenty years.*

Bill was a handsome boy of fourteen, full of animal spirits and
deviltry.

More often than not, he managed to keep Mary's whole class-
room in a titter and Mary on the verge of tears, for it was hard to
get even the minimum amount of work out of her pupils with his
distracting influence.

One morning Mary told God about Bill. Then she wrote a
prayer in shorthand and slipped it into her Bible.

At that moment Bill himself appeared in the door, and, like a
friendly dog mischievously wagging his tail, he stopped in front of
her desk.

"What are you writing, Miss Mary?"

"Something I want God to do for me," she replied calmly.

"You think God can read shorthand?"

"I think God can do anything—even answer that prayer!"
Mary said vehemently.

Bill's curiosity was challenged. He could not stop thinking about that note written to God in shorthand. After class he slipped back into the room, took the bit of paper from the Bible, and went around the corner of the schoolhouse to look at it.

All he could read was his own name. But he kept the note and put it in the back of his typing book.

The years went by and Bill grew into manhood. Eventually he entered a successful law practice, married, and became the father of two children. He still pursued his irresponsible, egocentric ways, just keeping on the safe side of disaster through luck and charm.

Then, after several years, his luck appeared to be on the wane. For the first time in his life, his home seemed to be on the verge of breakup. People were getting wise to Bill.

In the midst of this personal turmoil, Bill's father died. Bill left immediately for the West Coast to be with his mother, where he remained until the family house had been disposed of. She was coming to live with him—another responsibility heaped onto those he could hardly cope with now.

As he went through old trunks and papers in his mother's attic, he came across something familiar, his old typing book.

As he thumbed through the yellowed pages, the memory of Miss Mary, tormented by his own provoking antics, came back to him. A slip of paper fell to the floor. With a start he recognized the prayer Miss Mary had written in shorthand.

What had she written about him? He seemed to hear, just as clearly as he had heard it that day in his boyhood, her sharp answer that God could do anything!

He took the worn bit of paper to his secretary and asked her to decipher it. As she read, an embarrassed expression came over her face, and he noticed that she blushed.

"It's a very personal message," she said. "I'd prefer to write it out and leave it on your desk."

He found it there when she had left for the day. The words stared up at him: "Dear God, don't let me fail this job. I cannot handle this class with Bill upsetting it. Touch his heart and make him a good boy. He's a boy who can be very great or very wicked."

The words struck hard. "Very great—or very wicked." For a long time Bill sat at his desk, thinking of his headlong years, trying to see himself as his harassed teacher, his distraught wife, his children, and his business associates must see him. It was dark when he left the office.

For days the message was like a living thing. It would not leave him. He kept it in his pocket and at intervals he took it out, reading it and rereading it.

Finally, in desperation, he decided to consult a minister.

"Do you believe that a prayer can be answered after twenty years?" he heard himself asking.

The minister smiled. "Sometimes God waits until the heart of a person is ready to receive it. And—the recipient of the blessing must do something to merit the answer," he replied.

Something of merit that he had done? He tried to think.

He had taken his mother to live with him at a time when his marriage was going on the rocks, when he wanted to evade the issue. Yet, after all, that was a small thing to do, all things considered. But—certainly it was one of the few unselfish things he had done during his whole life....

His thoughts began to clear just slightly. It was as if a door opened and a ray of light tried desperately to come through. He considered. Thoughtfully, slowly but very surely, he made his decision: He would go back and make his marriage a success.

They talked for a long time, Bill and the minister, and Bill went away with an inner peace that he had not known before. From that day, his whole life changed. Today, Bill is on the way to becoming "very great."

Months later he sent a letter to his old teacher, who is my sister. As she read it, a light came into her eyes.

"Yes," she said. "I do believe that God answers every prayer."

The Yellow Kite

BEVERLY NEWMAN

Slowly, depression had got her, and she was sinking into premature old age. Meanwhile, her marriage was beginning to fall apart. As for God, why should He care about such a condition?

I stood at the window and watched the neighborhood children on the hill behind our house flying their kites. My four-year-old son, Michael, stood next to me with his face eagerly pressed against the glass. Then, looking up at me with pleading eyes, he again asked if he could have a kite like the other children.

For days now, ever since he had first seen them congregate on the hill, Michael had been asking the same question, and I had given him the same answer: "Wait until you are a little older."

It was easier not to go into a long explanation, but actually Michael was too young to fly a kite all by himself, which meant that one of his parents would always have to go with him to help. Because of my health I simply didn't have the strength or energy, and my husband was usually at work. Once again, Michael hid his face in my skirt, something he always did when he was going to cry and didn't want me to see.

As I turned from the window, I felt like crying myself. I looked around the room; the furniture was shabby and worn, and the walls were badly in need of paint. You could see the light places on them, the spots where previous tenants had hung their pictures. Even though we had lived here for several months, I had not done very much to fix up the place. We had moved so many times, and each time it seemed like the neighborhood was a little more run-down, and the houses a little older, each one in need of repairs.

My husband, Bill, worked long, irregular hours at his job and earned a good salary. However, we never seemed to have enough money, and we kept going deeper in debt. I had lost three children through miscarriages, and the complications that followed had required several emergency trips to the hospital and the constant care of a doctor. As a result, a tension had grown between Bill and me, and we found we could no longer get along with one another.

It all looked so hopeless; even God seemed to have forgotten us. I prayed so often about our problems, asking God for help, but things only seemed to get worse. I found myself thinking, *God doesn't care, and I guess I don't either.*

I walked over to the mirror and studied my reflection. I thought I was looking at a stranger. I looked pale and worn, much older than my years. I no longer bothered to fix my face or do anything with my hair. I stepped back and studied my whole image—the old dress that I had worn all week was wrinkled and torn at the pocket, and there was a button missing at the neck.

As I stood there and stared at myself, a feeling of dread, almost panic, came over me, and it filled my whole body with fear. It was the realization that I was giving up on life. I had stopped caring about anything; I felt defeated. I could no longer rise above the depression that had taken hold of me.

In the last few months, my husband had grown rather quiet. We did not talk much. I was aware of his eyes studying me when he thought I was preoccupied with something. I used to be so particular about everything. Bill had not said a word about the change that had come over me, but his actions said a lot. He made a special effort to get me interested in new things, but I did not respond. In fact, I did not respond to him in any way, and he did not know quite how to handle me anymore.

Michael was the one spark of life left for me. He could make me smile, and when he hugged me, I would feel love. I clung to him much in the way one would cling to a life preserver. He needed me and I knew it—that kept me going.

When I tucked him into bed that evening, Michael said, "Mommy, may I pray to God to send me a yellow kite?" Then, fearing that I might again repeat what I had said so many times before, he added, "Maybe He doesn't think I'm too young."

"Yes," I said. "We will leave it up to Him to decide about it once and for all." I was tired of the whole thing and hoped that maybe this would make Michael stop talking about it.

Michael prayed his prayer and fell asleep with a smile on his face. As I stood there looking down at that beautiful child with blond curls, so trusting in his faith that God would answer his little prayer, I found myself questioning God. Would He really answer such a small prayer when He had chosen not to hear any of my frantic pleas or send me any help to relieve my situation? "Oh, God," I prayed, "please help me! Show me the way out of this dark place."

The next morning as I raised the shade in the kitchen, I stared at the sight that met my eyes—a string hanging down in front of the window. Not quite able to believe the thoughts that were assembling in my mind, I found myself running out the back door and into the yard. There it was: a yellow kite caught on the roof with its string hanging down.

"Oh, thank You, God, thank You!" I repeated over and over

again. I was thanking Him for the yellow kite, and I was thanking Him for the joy that was flooding into my soul. He had answered the prayer of a little boy, just a little prayer, but by answering that prayer, He had also answered my prayer for help.

Suddenly I remembered Michael. I ran to his room, scooped him up in my arms and carried him into the backyard. He was still half-asleep and didn't quite know what to make of this mother who was babbling about something on the roof and saying, "Wait until you see!"

He clapped his hands and bounced up and down in my arms when he saw the kite. "Mommy, Mommy, and it's even yellow!" he exclaimed. I smiled at him and added, "It's a miracle, too." He hugged me and said, "I knew God would answer my prayer. I just knew He would."

I thought to myself, *This was why I had been so depressed. I had lost my faith. I had turned my back on God and then insisted that He had stopped caring.* The yellow kite was not the only miracle that God sent to us that morning.

When Bill came home we took the kite to the beach and flew it. It went so high that it was almost out of sight for a while. Bill said he had never seen a kite fly as high. We asked all over the neighborhood but never could find a trace of the kite's former owner.

We moved several times in the years that followed, and the yellow kite always went with us. My depression left me and as my health improved, so did my relationship with my husband.

At each new place I would hang the kite in some corner where I could see it as I went about my duties. It served as a reminder that no matter how bad things may seem, we must never lose sight of the fact that God cares, that He hears our prayers. No request is too big or too small to bring before Him.

Lost

GRACE WATERS

The storm caught the girls out in the open. In their fear, they ran and ran—until they were completely lost. What should they do?

❧

"We must hurry home from school this afternoon," said Dorothy. "It looks as if it is going to rain."

"Yes, and we have to go to the big pasture to get the cows tonight too," added Carol.

Dorothy and Carol were ten and twelve years of age, respectively. They enjoyed being in the country, even though they missed having their father with them, for Mr. Brown worked in the city and could come home only occasionally. The family lived on a small tract of land, the back part of which was wooded. It was here that Mr. Brown pastured his few cows.

When Carol and Dorothy arrived home, they changed their school clothes for work clothes and at once began helping their mother prepare supper. There was no time to play, for there was much to be done.

After supper was over and the dishes were put away, Mother said, "Girls, you must start after the cows now, so that I will have time to milk them before dark. Hurry, for it won't be long now."

Away they ran for caps and coats, and started over the hill toward the pasture.

By this time the sky was quite dark and was getting darker every minute. They hurried as fast as they could, but when they arrived at the gate, the cows were not there. Carol called, and Dorothy called, only to hear their voices echo and reecho through the woods. They listened, but they did not hear any cowbells.

"Well," said Carol, "I guess there is nothing to do but go and look for them."

Dorothy was more hesitant. "What if it is dark before we get back?" she queried.

"Oh, we'll hurry," reassured the older girl.

Saying this, Carol started along the narrow path, which led up over the hill and down on the other side into the back part of the pasture. Dorothy followed obediently.

All this time it was getting darker. It began to rain. In the distance could be heard the roll of thunder, which was becoming louder and more distinct. The rain poured down in torrents for several minutes. By this time, it had become so dark that the girls could hardly see the path in front of them. Then suddenly it stopped raining, and the stars and the moon began to shine.

"I think I hear the bell over this way," said Dorothy.

"No, I think it is that way," Carol replied, pointing in the opposite direction. "Perhaps we should go home and get some help."

And so they turned back and walked what seemed to them twice the distance to the gate. Still no gate was in sight.

Dorothy had not known that there could possibly be so many queer noises in the woods. In the distance an owl hooted, and right over their heads his mate answered. This so startled the girls that they began to run, scaring a little rabbit from behind a bush. The

rabbit was so frightened that he, too, ran—right between the two girls. This frightened them still more, so that they ran until they were exhausted. Then they sat down on a nearby log to rest and to think what to do next. They decided to go on.

But there were other things besides rabbits and owls to frighten them. They began thinking of the stories they had heard of the wild animals that roamed those woods. There were bears, coyotes, and sometimes cougars. Carol and Dorothy did not want to meet any of these that night. Every few minutes they would look behind them to see if some animal might be following them.

Quite often they would hear the bushes crack, and then they would start running again. But, for all of this, they saw no animals. The recent rain had caused the ground to become soft, and very often while they were walking or running, their feet would sink in the mud.

Finally, they stopped and sat down to rest again. They were getting cold, their clothes were wet, and they were very tired.

After resting awhile, Carol exclaimed, "Why, Dorothy, this is the very spot where we were when we decided to go home."

"It is, isn't it? We must be lost then." And Dorothy began to cry at the very thought of their not being able to find their way home. "What shall we do? We can't stay here all night."

By this time Carol was afraid, too, but she dared not show it. She must be brave before her little sister. "Let's pray," she said. "Jesus has always answered our prayers before, and I am sure He will do it this time. Mother says Jesus likes to have us pray to Him."

And so they knelt down right there where they were and asked God to help them find their way home. And besides this, they told the Lord that they wanted to see their father, who had been away on a business trip for two weeks.

When they arose and looked around, Carol pointed straight in front of them, and said, "Look, Dorothy, at that big tree over there, the biggest one. Isn't that that big tree just a little way from the gate?"

"I don't know, but it certainly looks like it. Let's go see." So they started, and soon they were at the gate.

"Dorothy, Jesus has answered our prayer already," said Carol happily. "I mean—the first part."

When they were almost home their mother met them, and although their clothes were dripping wet, Mrs. Brown threw her arms around both of her daughters and gave each of them a big hug and kiss. As they started to the house, she asked, "Girls, what has taken you so long? We have all been worrying about you. Mr. Smith said that he found the cows over in his field. He brought them home, and they are all milked. Two of the neighbors are out looking for you, now. They have been looking for you for almost an hour."

Then the girls told of all their experiences and how they found their way home.

"Now, hurry and get into some dry clothes. I have a surprise for you," smiled Mother.

"We already know what the surprise is, and we want to go in and see Father first," Carol cried.

"Well, how did you know that Father was here?" Mother asked, with a puzzled look on her face.

"Oh, that's the second part," answered Dorothy.

"The what?" asked Mother, as the girls vanished into the parlor.

"Of our prayer," Carol called back.

That evening was a happy one for the entire Brown family. Father and Mother were glad that their daughters had discovered the possibilities of prayer, and Dorothy and Carol were glad to be home with Mother and Father and to know for themselves that God hears and answers prayers that even juniors offer.

Please, God, Save Our Amy!

LOIS OLSON

Holding Amy in her arms, she began to pray.
There was no other hope but God.

How many coincidences does it take to add up to a miracle? I never gave much thought to that question until one terrifying autumn day.

It was September 1975, and the nights were already getting cold in the isolated valley of the North Cascade Mountains in Washington State where we lived. My husband, Tom, taught school in the little village of Stehekin, accessible to the outside world only by a four-hour ferryboat ride across Lake Chelan, or a half-hour flight in a pontoon plane when the weather permits planes to fly. No roads over the rugged mountains. No telephones. Nothing.

Tom taught in a one-room schoolhouse built of logs where our eight-year-old, Sally, was the only third-grader among twelve pupils. Having had some teaching experience back in Ohio, I often helped Tom around the school, and on this day I had brought along our four-year-old, Amy.

The older kids were playing baseball. Amy got excited and suddenly ran in front of the batter just as he swung. The bat struck her on the right side of the head. Numb with fright, I examined her. Blood was dripping from her ear.

As upset and concerned as two parents could be, Tom and I rushed Amy in our old car to a retired physician, the only doctor in the village, who cleaned and dressed the wound. "She should be all right," he said. I hoped with all my heart that this was true, because we had nowhere else to turn.

Tom went back to school, and the doctor's wife drove Amy and me back to our home, deep in the woods, five miles from the village. "Are you sure it's all right for me to leave you here?" she asked.

"I think so," I said. Amy appeared to be alert, her head was bandaged, and there seemed no reason for the doctor's wife to stay. But soon after she left, when I tried to change Amy's bloody shirt, she could not move her arms to help.

I was terrified. I knew that something was desperately wrong with my child. I had no telephone, no car. Even at the village there was no hospital, no medical facility. It would be hours before Tom came home.

Holding Amy in my arms, I began to pray. I prayed because I had no other source of help or strength. I had always believed in God, but I was not certain of the extent to which He would go to help me. I had been told about His glory and power, but had not really felt them touch my life since my childhood, when I had recovered from a polio siege. Now I called on Him with every ounce of strength in me.

I knew that I had to get help for Amy somehow. So I began walking down the road. The boat landing was five miles away, and Amy weighed forty pounds. My back had been damaged by polio, and I didn't know how far I could go. As I walked, I kept praying.

Amy lay limp in my arms. Suddenly she looked up and said, in a strange, slurred voice, "Wha ah we ooing, Mama?" Amy had always expressed herself clearly for a four-year-old. Now her speech was so slurred that I could hardly understand her. I had worked with retarded children and knew this might be a sign of brain damage. I tried to walk faster. I even tried to run, but my strength was ebbing. *"God, please!"* I cried over the pounding of my heart.

Exactly at that moment a car turned onto the road from a side road up ahead. But it was heading away from us, toward the village. I screamed, "Help! Help!" as loud as I could. But the car kept going and disappeared around a curve.

I was crying now, tears of hopelessness and despair. Then I heard the car stop. I began running and shouting again. I heard the car start up again; it then appeared around the curve, backing up.

It was my friend and distant neighbor, Rhoda Fellows. "Lois! What's happened?" she gasped.

"I've got to get Amy to a doctor," I cried. As we flew along the twisty road I told Rhoda what had happened. "It's strange," she said. "I wasn't sure I heard a call, and I almost never go into the village at this time." She drove us to the school because I knew Tom would want to be with us, and I needed him. Then she sped off to the boat landing to radio for a plane to come quickly.

As she left, another car pulled into the schoolyard. It was the ride home for the up-valley children. Somehow the man had come early and was able to take charge of the other students so Tom could leave.

As we drove to the landing—Tom and our daughter Sally and I—Amy started trembling. Convulsive jerks contorted her left side and her tongue clacked against her mouth. I fought down panic as I realized that she was having a brain seizure. My only shred of hope lay in the fact that she was still conscious.

Tom and Sally and I began praying: "Our Father, who art in heaven…" As we prayed, I looked at Amy, lying in my lap, and I saw that she was praying, too—mouthing the words along with us in jerks and slurs and sounds.

"Thy will be done, on earth as it is in heaven…" Now Amy's lips barely moved, but I knew that her spirit was calling to God. I remembered how we had taught her the Lord's Prayer when she could barely talk, remembered how she would say it every night, and the thought came to me that if any prayer could be heard by a merciful God and answered, it was Amy's. I had to fight back tears as I looked at her. Then, suddenly, Amy lapsed into unconsciousness and slumped limply in my arms.

At this moment my panic should have been complete, but somehow in that moment of prayer, my daughter's prayer, my own faith in God had been heightened and strengthened as never before in my life. My heart was pounding, but deep inside there was a feeling of calm that can come only from God.

When we arrived at the landing, a gale was blowing. Tom raced off to the radio to find out if the plane was coming and was told it was doubtful, the weather was so bad. We also found that the daily ferry had been delayed; it should have left long ago.

"There's a doctor on the ferry," someone said. "He stayed at the lodge last night."

"Oh, where is he? Where is he?" I begged. The gusts of wind were so strong I had to brace myself against them.

Tom came running up from the landing and took Amy from my sagging arms. "Ernie's going to try to make it," he said. Ernie was the airplane pilot, a brave and capable flier.

"There's a doctor on the ferry," I told Tom. "Let's try to find him."

Tom ran with Amy toward the boat and was met at the gang-plank by a bearded, gray-haired man. We placed Amy on the back seat of a station wagon and the doctor climbed in and examined her. She was still unconscious and her breathing was now more labored and very rapid. The doctor turned to Tom. "I'll be right back," he said. He hurried back on the ferry and returned with another man.

"This is Doctor Dwiggens," he said. "We are colleagues at Stanford Medical Center, and I didn't know he was here until we met on the ferry a few moments ago. He's just the man you need."

I didn't understand why he was, but in the next half-hour I found out. Doctor Dwiggens was a respiratory specialist who knew exactly what to do for Amy, and he worked frantically to keep her breathing.

I leaned over the seat and talked to Amy, hoping she could hear me. Tom put his arm around her and stroked her pale cheek, tears streaming down his face. The people from the village and the ferry passengers gathered around in uneasy little groups, many of them praying.

For half an hour we waited for the small seaplane, bucking its way against the wind, to reach us. The ferry stayed at the landing, waiting to see if Ernie could make it. At last we heard the sound of the plane as it broke through the scudding clouds and swooped low over the choppy lake. We held our breaths as the crest of waves tore at the pontoons. The plane bounced and tossed, but stayed upright and afloat. Ernie had made it! One of the old-timers shook his head. "Only a pilot with thirty years of experience could have done that," he said.

Suddenly Amy regained consciousness and began to cry. It was the most beautiful sound I've ever heard! All around me I could hear people saying, "Thank God."

Doctor Dwiggens, Sally, Amy, Tom, and I squeezed into the little plane. After a perilous flight in high winds and a thirty-five-mile ambulance ride to the Wenatchee Hospital, Amy underwent surgery. She had suffered a deep skull fracture. Five bone splinters were removed from her skull, but none had penetrated the delicate membrane protecting her brain.

Today, Amy has full use of all her limbs and faculties, and speaks as clearly as she did before the accident.

How many coincidences does it take to add up to a miracle? I still don't know. But I do know that with Rhoda Fellows' car being in just the right place at the right time, the ferry being detained with just the doctor we needed, the courage of the only pilot who could have set that plane down on that storm-tossed lake, and finally the miracle of Amy's undamaged brain—no one will ever be able to tell me that those things could have taken place without God's special intervention and guidance. He gave our little girl back to us. And we'll praise Him for it every day of our lives.

The Hand on My Shoulder

JERRY BOND

The house was on fire, and a little girl was in terrible danger. He had to help her somehow—but what if he chose the wrong room? In seconds, it might be too late! So, in desperation, he prayed for help.

Help came in the flames. A hand...and a voice.

Late one March evening in 1974, I was awakened by the sound of distant cries and shouts. At first I thought it was a domestic quarrel, but an urgency in the voices caused me to think it might be something else. I got up and opened the window. The smell of smoke, heavy and pungent, drifted into the room. And the voices, shrill with panic, cut clearly through the cool night air.

"Help me! Help me! My little girl is in there!"

Alarmed, I pulled on my pants, grabbed a flashlight and followed the cries to Medlin Street, a block and a half away. There the house of a family named Green, a one-story brick structure, was ablaze. Black smoke was pouring out of the windows. A small crowd had gathered, mostly neighbors and a few policemen. The fire department hadn't arrived yet.

In the flickering orange-black darkness, I watched in horror as a team of men worked to pull Mr. Green, severely burned and in a state of shock, through a small window near the back of the house. Then I saw Mrs. Green and three of her children huddled together on the front lawn. Their faces mirrored fear and terror. Mrs. Green was hysterical.

"Theresa!" she screamed. "My Theresa is still in there!"

I've got to do something, I thought. *I've got to help.* But I stood there frozen, unable to move. Confusion and panic surrounded me, became a part of me. The whole atmosphere seemed to crackle with heat and tension. I was afraid. A great shower of fiery sparks lit the night sky as part of the house caved in, and I heard Mrs. Green scream again.

"Oh, Lord," I prayed. "Please help me." And then I rushed to the house and pushed my way through the first available window. Once inside, I could hardly see. My heart was beating like a drum. Everything was black and smoking.

I groped my way forward until I got halfway across the room. Then, abruptly, I stopped. Something—some strong and strange sensation—told me that I was in the wrong room. *This isn't right,* it seemed to say. *This isn't where you'll find her.* The feeling was so powerful that I couldn't shake it. And then I felt on my shoulder the sure, firm grasp of a hand pulling me back toward the window.

"Get out of here!" I yelled, fearing for the other person's safety. I turned to follow, but there was no one. There was only myself, alone and trembling.

Gasping, I headed for the window, pulled myself through, and lowered myself to the ground. I looked up to see Mrs. Green's frantic eyes desperately searching my own for encouragement. Finding none, she gestured wildly toward another window.

"There," she whispered hoarsely. "Go in *there!*"

The window was a few feet off the ground. Someone gave me

a boost, and I pushed myself inside, dropping to the floor with a thud. This room, too, was dark and smoldering. My eyes were smarting. I could barely see an arm's length ahead.

"Oh, Lord," I prayed again, "please help me."

What happened next left me momentarily stunned. First, as if in answer to my prayer, I felt a surge of confidence that I was, indeed, in the right place, that I would find Theresa. And then, to my amazement, I felt the return of the same firm force on my shoulder that had pulled me from the other room. This time, however, it was even stronger and it seemed to push me to the floor. Though I didn't understand what was happening, I didn't fight it. Instinctively, I let it take over. Its presence was both calming and reassuring. I knew it was good.

I relaxed and let myself be pushed to the floor. I began to crawl, following the wall, arms outstretched, reaching, grabbing. I came to a bed and raised myself to search its rumpled surface. *No!* a voice seemed to warn. *Stay low!* I returned to my crawling position. I had found nothing on the bed. *Don't worry,* the voice whispered. *You're almost there. Don't worry.*

At the foot of the bed lay a great pile of charred chairs, quilts and blankets that seemed to have been thrown to the floor by someone in a panic. Reaching deep into the tangled maze, I found what I had been looking for—an arm, a leg, it was impossible to tell—but I knew I had found Theresa. I pulled and pulled until she finally emerged, a limp brown-haired bundle. She was badly burned.

"Theresa?" I whispered.

A shuddering gasp, barely audible, confirmed that she was alive. I threw her over my shoulder and ran for the window.

The crowd outside stared in silence as I gently laid Theresa on the ground and began to administer mouth-to-mouth resuscitation. Her small face, black with soot and burns, was expressionless. Blue lights from police cars pulsated in the darkness. As I breathed into her tiny frame, I prayed for her survival. Wailing sirens and flashing red lights announced the arrival of fire trucks. I kept on breathing into her mouth and praying. I listened to the fire chief bellowing orders on his bullhorn, and then I heard the front door being kicked in. The fire, reignited by the fresh supply of oxygen, exploded with a scorching blast. Theresa's eyelids fluttered. She was breathing on her own. I held her until the ambulance arrived.

"Looks like you got her out just in time," said the medic, as he took her from my arms. "She's burned pretty bad, but she'll be all right."

I waited for the ambulance to pull away before returning home. Shaken by the experience, plagued by the smell of burning flesh and the echoes of terrified screams, I couldn't sleep. More than anything else, I was completely unnerved by the mysterious Presence that had led me to the little girl. I had always had faith in God and in the power of prayer, but this kind of intervention seemed uncanny, too close for comfort—at least for me. The idea was too much to comprehend, but I couldn't dismiss it. It kept me up all night.

At 7 A.M., I put on a jacket and shoes and returned to the scene of the fire. The house, a charred hull of blackened brick, was still smoldering. Skeletal shells of smoking furniture were strewn around the front yard. The fire inspector was there with a few policemen. He asked me what I was doing there. I told him. He said the blaze had probably been caused by a cigarette left burning on the living room sofa.

I went around to the room where I had found Theresa. Like the rest of the house, it was badly charred and blackened from smoke. The walls were blistered from the intense heat. In one corner rested the remains of a melted tennis racket.

Slowly I turned to gaze around the gutted room, when suddenly I stopped, transfixed—my eyes riveted on the wall. There, directly above the spot where I had found Theresa, was a portrait, neatly hung and, strangely, the only thing in the room undamaged by the fire. The frame, to be sure, was black with soot, but the face, the calm, steady, reassuring face, was clear and untouched.

It was a picture of Jesus.

To this day, I don't know how long I stood there, incredulously returning the portrait's gaze. But when I left, it was with newfound understanding that I whispered my thanks.

EPILOGUE

O LORD, you have examined my heart
and know everything about me.
You know when I sit down or stand up.
You know my every thought when far away.
You chart the path ahead of me
and tell me where to stop and rest.
Every moment you know where I am.
You know what I am going to say
even before I say it, LORD....
You place your hand of blessing
on my head....

You watched me as I was being
formed in utter seclusion,
as I was woven together in the dark
of the womb.
You saw me before I was born.
Every day of my life was recorded in
your book.
Every moment was laid out
before a single day had passed.

PSALM 139:1-5, 15-16 (NLT)

Years before I came across that mind-boggling 139th Psalm, I was convinced that God was choreographing my life. The epiphany occurred at the end of a sabbatical I took in 1982. Looking back at those months of travel and research, it suddenly

hit me, in almost as blinding a light as Saul/Paul experienced on
the way to Damascus:

> How can this be? I had this long trip planned to a T: I knew
> where I was going, how long it would take me to get there,
> where I was going to stay, how long I would remain in each
> place, what I would accomplish there, and what I would
> accomplish altogether.
>
> Now I belatedly discover that I was not my own choreo-
> grapher after all. Behind the scenes, God, the Grand Chess-
> master of the Universe, the Supreme Dramatist, had
> choreographed me on a script I knew not of. Where I
> planned research, God planned an O. Henry twist ending,
> warping me out of workaholism into service for His lambs.
> While I did accomplish a significant amount of research, it
> could not begin to compare to the ministry to suffering
> humanity set up for me by God.

My life has never been the same since.

I have seen it happen over and over and over: God's split-
second timing—one second less or one second more and a meeting
would not have taken place. Each day I am on the road, am speaking, or am signing books, I ask my Divine Choreographer to bring
to me (or me to them) every soul He wishes me to touch. He *does*.
Since my Damascus experience in 1982, I have been catapulted
out of my self-centered ruts into the golden pathway of God's grace
and leading. The first casualty was self—and I have rarely missed
Him since.

God Put You on This Train!

JOSEPH LEININGER WHEELER

*I was a complaining Jonah, totally undeserving
of the blessings God had in store for me.*

I have always loved trains. Indeed, interwoven into the very fabric
of my childhood and growing-up years are the sights, smells,
sounds, and sensations of trains: the hissing of steam-powered
locomotives; the clang of the bell; the *clackety-clack, clackety-clack*
theme song when on board; the wail of the old-time engine, which
even this day sends chills up and down my spine when I hear it or
remember it; the people who ride on these rails and who generally
come into my life, become friends, get off, and walk out of my life
forever.

Thus, when the opportunity came to board an eastbound
Amtrak train a few years ago, I felt a surge of joy within me, a joy I
rarely experience on interstate freeways or on transcontinental air-
liners.

After boarding in Montana, I found my row, leaned back in
my seat, and immersed myself in the experience of train. The blasting air horn way up ahead was a good sound, but it was nothing at
all like the remembered wail of the old-time locomotives—oh, not
even close!

Day turned into night, and night turned into day, as we clackety-clacked eastward. I made new friends, I dreamed, I read, I thought, I regenerated.

*And then...*I began to worry about my speaking appointment in western New York. It was the summer of the great Mississippi floods, you see, and the news ahead was anything but good: If we made it across at all, we would most likely be the last train to do so, for some time to come. Rumors swept up and down the aisles of the long silver snake. Some maintained we'd make it across, others that we might, others that we wouldn't—and all through-passengers were deeply concerned about how and when they'd get to their destinations.

Finally, over the loudspeakers came the verdict. There was near-total silence, except for an occasional baby cry, as we were given the news: the train *could not* make it across—the river was already too wide, and getting wider every moment. Amtrak personnel would be coming through the train to speak with all through-passengers. And they were dreadfully sorry for the inconvenience. That was all. Hubbub followed, everyone talking at once, the soundtrack complete with laughter, anger, tears—as well as the unmistakably frightened high voices of children. I've never experienced anything else quite like it.

At last, an Amtrak official entered our car, and all conversation ground to a halt. Rather than talk to all of us at once, he merely turned to those in the front seats, and then worked his way back. Since I was at the back, it took some time for him to reach me.

"Well, sir, how far are you going, and are you on a tight schedule? In other words, do you have any appointments you have to make, or are you flexible in terms of us rerouting you?"

I certainly had not the luxury of being rerouted, and I told him

why, as well as when and where I was due in western New York. The upshot of it all was that I was taken off the train at the next sizable town, flown across raging "Old Man River" to O'Hare Airport in Chicago, shuttled to the train station downtown, and placed on board a train heading for New York.

By now I was anything but the proverbial "happy camper." I was royally irked. Worst of all, there was no one on whom I could take out my frustrations: Amtrak had lost plenty of money on me, and the Mississippi was safe from any puny retaliation from my corner. So, since insurance adjusters label such weather-induced disasters "acts of God," peevishly I took it out on Him.

Compounding my wrath was the microscopic little "stateroom"—barely big enough for me to turn around in!—that I had been assigned. I needed a shoehorn to insert my suitcase, hanging bag, cowboy hat, and multitudinous books, and close the sliding door. Shortly afterward, the train jerked into motion and eased its way out of the station and then the city. It was now night.

Then, there was a knock on the door.

Irritated, with a what-else-can-possibly-happen-to-me-now look on my face, I unlocked the door and opened it wide. There in the aisle stood the porter. Directly across from me, a polished young woman slid open her door. I had met her boarding the train, and she had been anything but friendly when I attempted to make small talk.

The porter told us he was there to instruct us as to the rules of the road, so to speak. We sat there in tandem, politely unresponsive. But he gave us his semicanned spiel nevertheless. Then he paused, curious. I must have appeared a strange sight to him: sitting on a cluttered bed (so short my head would touch one wall, and my feet the other), and my hand holding up a canvas bag stuffed with books perched precariously on the commode (the only place I had found to put it on), and a big black hat jutting out from a shelf. As fate would have it, the book on top was my *Remote Controlled*. "What's that all about?" he questioned. I proceeded to tell him about the thirty years of media research that went into it. Since he was concerned about the effects of television on his children, he forgot the rest of his passengers and leaped into an intense and sometimes emotional discussion. About twenty minutes later, he chanced to look down at his watch, and sputtered to a stop. Promising to speak with me further on the matter, he moved on.

For some unexplainable reason, all during this discussion, the door across the aisle had remained open, although the young woman there had contributed not a word. Now I looked across at her in the sudden stillness and wondered what to say. In a quiet, well-modulated voice, she asked if that was the only book I had written. Her question led us into an entirely different direction, to my anthologies of Christmas stories. By then, she had told me of her interest in music, psychology, drama, and literature, and her advanced university study. Offhand-like, she asked me, "Do you have a story you've written in one of those books that I could read?" Swiftly, my mind ranged through the stories, then concluded that, with her interest in music and literature, probably she'd enjoy most "'Meditation' in a Minor Key."

"But it's a *long* story," I warned her.

"I don't care," she sighed resignedly, "what else do I have to do?"

So I dug down into the bag of books, pulled out *Christmas in My Heart, Volume 1*, and passed it across the aisle to her. Not knowing her at all, not even knowing if she was a Christian, I told her nothing of the story's origins, of the fact that twice during its writing I had come to a dead end, and each time I had given up, tossed the story into God's lap, and petulantly groused: "I've come as far with this story as I can go, and Joe Wheeler can take it no further! If it's Your will that it be completed, *You'll* have to take it from here!" In each case, at my inner door the next morning was a celestial fax. "Oh, so that's the way it should go!" I'd exclaim in joy, and move on with the story. That's the reason I've always told reporters that the Lord cowrote that story. But I didn't tell her that. Not then.

After scanning the book, she came to "Meditation" and began reading it. She said not a word but merely stared intently at the print, and occasionally turned a page. Meanwhile, I was ill at ease: *That was one long story! What was I supposed to be doing while she read it? She hadn't purchased it, so it was still my book.* I ended up doing nothing. I just sat there in my stateroom, scanning my own books in a desultory fashion, muttering things to my inner self.

After what seemed forever—but it was probably no more than three-quarters of an hour—across the aisle the pages ceased to be turned. She just sat there motionless. Finally, I concluded ruefully, *I've put her to sleep,* and got up, walked across the swaying train aisle to find out for sure—only to discover that tears were streaming down her cheeks. She literally was incapable of speech. I handed her my handkerchief, and she wiped away the tears that just kept coming.

In time, the tears ceased—and the floodgates opened and torrents of words rushed through. They did not ebb until around 2 A.M. We soon decided to vacate our narrow quarters in favor of the diner. There, for a time, we were joined by the porter—but most of the time we were alone together. She told me, in capsulized form, the sad, dark, unhappy story of her life. How her life was a dead end, how all her romantic relationships had been failures, how her career track appeared to be sterile and lacking in fulfillment, how she had lost faith in God, how she had increasingly wondered if life was even worth living, and how—on a mere whim—she had decided to board this train, hoping that on it somehow, some way, she might come up with solutions, answers, and so avoid the unthinkable.

Gradually, as the hours fled by, her face began to lose its hardness as a new softness came into her eyes, a new sense of purpose, a new willingness to accept God back into her life, a new joy.

Her last words as we said good-bye to each other—she was getting off early in the morning—were, "Oh! What if God hadn't put you on this train!"

I was a long time in getting to sleep, rethinking the drama of that evening, and how mightily the Lord had used my frail words to bring a wandering child back into the circle of His love.

The next morning, I got off the train at Syracuse, rented a car, and headed toward the Finger Lakes region for my afternoon speaking appointment. I got lost several times and had to stop in the increasing heat to ask directions. By midday it had soared past one hundred degrees. In my discomfort, like Elijah of old, I forgot my mountaintop experience of the day before and began to pout and complain à la Jonah. Looking back on that day, I wonder how it was possible for me to forget so soon how mightily the Lord had led and blessed only hours before. But it was so.

Eventually I arrived at the lakeside retreat where I was to speak in the midafternoon. When I got out of the car, it felt like I had just stepped into a furnace. The grass was withering under the blasting heat, and I was to speak during the hottest part of the afternoon—*in a tent!* By now, my Jonah act had hit full stride, and I was venting my anger and discomfort inwardly, angling it second-hand up to the good Lord, whom I snarlingly held at least partly responsible.

After I walked up to the information booth, wiped the sweat off my face, and introduced myself, the gentleman running it sighed in relief, saying, "Oh, Dr. Wheeler, am I glad to see *you!* We were worrying that you weren't going to make it! And there is a gentleman who has been looking for you all day—says it's *urgent.* Let's see if I can take you to—oh, here he comes now!"

There he came indeed, hurrying across the lawn toward me, heat or no heat. I did not recognize him at all. As soon as he found out who I was, he told me to stay right there as he had something to bring me; then he puffed away in the direction of his tent. Soon, he was back, carrying in his hand one of my books. I murmured to myself, *All this fuss over a mere autograph?*

And then he told me the story. His only sister (young, vivacious, happily married to a man she loved, and having four small children)…he paused to gain control, then, brokenly, he told me she was dying of an incurable disease. At most, she had two weeks left to live! Being one of my former students, she had entrusted her brother with this one responsibility: Travel some considerable distance to this retreat—for she had read I was going to be there—"and get Dr. Wheeler to inscribe this book to me, and get it back to me before I die."

The rest of that fateful afternoon is sort of a blur to me now. I know I inscribed a copy of each of my books to her and her family, vainly searching for words that would be commensurate with the occasion and the effort it took to get the book to me. Her brother, his shoulders heaving, and eyes wet, took my hand in a viselike grip, and said, "Oh, thank God you came! I don't know how I could have gone back to my sister without your inscription!"

Then we hugged and he strode quickly away to pack his car. He had made the long trip for that one reason alone; now he was returning to his sister, hoping and praying he would get there in time. He did.

I spoke later that afternoon in a slightly ragged, and thoroughly chastened, voice. I don't remember what I said. But I *do* remember I shared this family's story, and agony, and that we prayed for her and her family.

Afterward, I could not face the well-wishers for very long, but escaped back to Syracuse to have it out with my soul. I could see, in retrospect, how my Lord and His angels had choreographed every step of my journey: Seconds off, and my life and ministry would never have included that troubled young woman who got on the train in Chicago; had I missed connections because of the flood, a heartbroken brother would have had to double the sorrow of his dying sister. And "Meditation" was not through yet: The next day, on the train to New York City, I sat next to a beautiful Ukrainian-American jet-setter. After philosophizing about life, God, and the meaning of it all for some time, she asked if she could read one of my stories. I can see that visual image yet: Outside the train window was the majestic Hudson River, and there she sat, reading. When she came to the end, she too was speechless. A lone tear trickled down her cheek. Then, unable to say anything, she gave me perhaps the ultimate tribute I have ever received as a writer: She leaned across and kissed me on the cheek.

My life has not been the same since that train trip. On it I gained a new sense of the fragility of life, and how quickly it can end. On it, I dumped my Jonah self out the window before the train drew in to Grand Central Station—I never want to see him again. But by far, most important of all, on it, God pulled back the curtains between me and heaven and revealed to my disbelieving eyes a great truth: Every day and night of my life, He and His angels are, behind the scenes, choreographing my every step, my every interaction.

Praise be to God for such divine condescension!

Acknowledgments

I am deeply indebted to my dear friend and story partner, Linda Steinke of Warburg, Alberta. She unearthed a number of these stories and is responsible for discovering W. A. Spicer's monumental treasure trove *The Hand That Intervenes;* two other cherished friends, Gar and Eleanor Baybrook of Leaves of Autumn Books in Payson, Arizona, found a copy of this old book and rushed it to me so I could access the 1918 text. Richard Coffen, vice president of editorial for Review and Herald Publishing Association, and Russell Holt, vice president for editorial for Pacific Press Publishing Association, were extremely helpful in facilitating story permissions. Anna Kanson, permissions director for Guideposts, went far beyond the call of duty to blitz the needed copyright permissions for stories originally published in *Guideposts* magazine. And, of course, the most indispensable persons of all, Erin Healy and Laura Barker, my editors at WaterBrook Press.

Introduction: "In the Shadow of His Wings," by Joseph Leininger
Wheeler. Copyright © 1998. Printed by permission of the author.

Section One: Surely He Shall Deliver Us

"He Shall Give His Angels Charge over You," by Lois Wheeler Berry.
Copyright © 1998. Printed by permission of the author and
Dorothy Johnson Muir.

"Led by Angels," by Muriel Parfitt. Published in *The Youth's Instructor*,
October 30, 1951. Reprinted by permission of Review and
Herald® Publishing Association, Hagerstown, Maryland 21740. If
anyone can provide knowledge of surviving Parfitt family, please
relay information to Joe Wheeler, care of WaterBrook Press.

"The Clock That Struck Thirteen," by W. A. Spicer. Published in
Spicer's book, *The Hand That Intervenes*, 1918. Text used by permis-
sion of Review and Herald® Publishing Association, Hagerstown,
Maryland 21740.

"Broken Chains, Open Doors," edited by W. A. Spicer. Published in
Spicer's book, *The Hand That Intervenes*, 1918. Text used by permis-
sion of Review and Herald® Publishing Association, Hagerstown,
Maryland 21740.

"Any Deadly Thing," by Marjorie Lewis Lloyd. Published in Lloyd's book,
It Must Have Been an Angel, 1978. Reprinted by permission of Pacific
Press Publishing Association, Nampa, Idaho, 83687. If anyone can
provide knowledge of the whereabouts of surviving Lloyd family,
please relay information to Joe Wheeler, care of WaterBrook Press.

"How Stanley Met Livingstone," by W. A. Spicer. Published in Spicer's
book, *The Hand That Intervenes*, 1918. Text used by permission of
Review and Herald® Publishing Association, Hagerstown, Maryland 21740.

"The Delayed Trial," by Marjorie Lewis Lloyd. Published in Lloyd's
book, *It Must Have Been an Angel*, 1978. Reprinted by permission
of Pacific Press Publishing Association, Nampa, Idaho 83687.

"An Angel Walked," by Lois M. Parker. Published in *The Youth's Instructor*, February 18, 1959. Reprinted by permission of Review and Herald® Publishing Association, Hagerstown, Maryland 21740. If anyone can provide knowledge of whereabouts of surviving Parker family, please relay information to Joe Wheeler, care of WaterBrook Press.

SECTION TWO: HE SHALL COVER US WITH HIS FEATHERS

"The Healing of Maude Blanford," by Catherine Marshall from *Guideposts*, April 1972. Reprinted with permission from *Guideposts* magazine. Copyright © 1972 by Guideposts, Carmel, New York 10512.

"An Indian Jonah," by W. A. Spicer and Bishop Whipple. Published in Spicer's book, *The Hand That Intervenes*, 1918. Text used by permission of Review and Herald® Publishing Association, Hagerstown, Maryland 21740.

"Too Strange to Be Coincidence," by Elizabeth Sherrill from *Guideposts*, November 1961. Reprinted with permission from *Guideposts* magazine. Copyright © 1961 by Guideposts, Carmel, New York 10512.

"Three Months in His Presence," by Virginia Lively from *Guideposts*, August 1966. Reprinted with permission from *Guideposts* magazine. Copyright © 1966 by Guideposts, Carmel, New York 10512.

"They Said I Didn't Have a Prayer," by George Shinn from *Guideposts*, January 1977. Reprinted with permission from *Guideposts* magazine. Copyright © 1977 by Guideposts, Carmel, New York 10512.

"Driven Far Off Course," edited by W. A. Spicer. Published in Spicer's book, *The Hand That Intervenes*, 1918. Text used by permission of Review and Herald® Publishing Association, Hagerstown, Maryland 21740.

"I'm Still Learning to Forgive," by Corrie ten Boom from *Guideposts*, November 1972. Reprinted with permission from *Guideposts* magazine. Copyright © 1972 by Guideposts, Carmel, New York 10512.

SECTION THREE: UNDER HIS WINGS WE SHALL TRUST

"Miracle Water," by Paula Cummings. Published in the *Guide*, July 26, 1978. Reprinted by permission of Review and Herald® Publishing Association, Hagerstown, Maryland 21740. If anyone can provide knowledge of the whereabouts of Paula Cummings or of her surviving family, please relay information to Joe Wheeler, care of WaterBrook Press.

"Food from the King's Table," by Stella Parker Peterson. Published in *The Youth's Instructor*, August 3, 1948. Reprinted by permission of Review and Herald® Publishing Association, Hagerstown, Maryland 21740.

"Praying for Shingles," by Marjorie Lewis Lloyd. Published in Lloyd's *It Must Have Been an Angel*, 1978. Reprinted by permission of Pacific Press Publishing Association, Nampa, Idaho 83687.

"Faith and Four Tables," by Fanny Lazzar from *Guideposts*, April 1971. Reprinted with permission from *Guideposts* magazine. Copyright © 1971 by Guideposts, Carmel, New York 10512.

"I Must Be in Quebec on Saturday Afternoon," by Charles Ingles. Published in Spicer's book, *The Hand That Intervenes*, 1918. Text used by permission of Review and Herald® Publishing Association, Hagerstown, Maryland 21740.

"The Miracle of Two Blue Coats," by B. Lyn Behrens. Published in the *Adventist Review*, September 1998. Reprinted by permission of Review and Herald® Publishing Association, Hagerstown, Maryland 21740, and B. Lyn Behrens, Loma Linda, California 92354.

"Soap and Bags and Hairs on My Head," by Wendy Miller. Copyright © 1997. Printed by permission of the author.

"Feeding the Orphans," by W. A. Spicer and A. T. Pierson. Published in Spicer's book, *The Hand That Intervenes*, 1918. Text used by permission of Review and Herald® Publishing Association, Hagerstown, Maryland 21740.

SECTION FOUR: HE SHALL GIVE HIS ANGELS CHARGE OVER US

"Gun in His Hand and Murder in His Heart," A Narrative of Early American Times. Published in Spicer's book, *The Hand That Intervenes*. Text used by permission of Review and Herald® Publishing Association, Hagerstown, Maryland 21740.

"Aunt Emma's Angel," by Florence Coleman. Published in *The Youth's Instructor*, November 28, 1939. Reprinted by permission of Review and Herald® Publishing Association, Hagerstown, Maryland 21740.

"The Angels of Chortiza," by Gwendolyn Lampshire Hayden. Published in *The Youth's Instructor*, May 6, 1952, as well as in Hayden's *Really Truly Stories, Book Seven*. Reprinted by permission of Review and Herald® Publishing Association, Hagerstown, Maryland 21740. If anyone can provide knowledge of the whereabouts of surviving Hayden family, please relay information to Joe Wheeler, care of WaterBrook Press.

"The Angel of the Lord," by Veldonna Jensen. Published in *The Youth's Instructor*, June 10, 1941. Reprinted by permission of Review and Herald® Publishing Association, Hagerstown, Maryland 21740. If anyone can provide knowledge of the whereabouts of surviving Jensen family, please relay information to Joe Wheeler, care of WaterBrook Press.

"Man on a White Horse," by John Jones and W. A. Spicer. Published in Spicer's book, *The Hand That Intervenes*, 1918. Text used by permission of Review and Herald® Publishing Association, Hagerstown, Maryland 21740.

"The Trembling Terror," by Marjorie Lewis Lloyd. Published in Lloyd's book, *It Must Have Been an Angel*, 1978. Reprinted by permission of Pacific Press Publishing Association, Nampa, Idaho 83867. If anyone can provide knowledge of the whereabouts of surviving Lloyd family, please relay information to Joe Wheeler, care of WaterBrook Press.

"Now You See Them," by Ruth Wheeler. Published in *It Must Have Been an Angel*, by Marjorie Lewis Lloyd, 1978. Reprinted by permission of Pacific Press Publishing Association, Nampa, Idaho 83687, and by Donald Wheeler, Takoma Park, Maryland 20912.

"When the Fire Went Out," by Louise Dubay and C. F. O'Dell. Published in *It Must Have Been an Angel*, by Marjorie Lewis Lloyd, 1978. Reprinted by permission of Pacific Press Publishing Association, Nampa, Idaho 83687. If anyone can provide knowledge of the whereabouts of Louise Dubay and C. F. O'Dell, please relay information to Joe Wheeler, care of WaterBrook Press.

"Angels Unawares," by Wanda Chilson. Published in *The Youth's Instructor*, September 21, 1937. Reprinted by permission of Review and Herald® Publishing Association, Hagerstown, Maryland 21740.

"Angels on Guard," by Von Asselt. Published in Spicer's book, *The Hand That Intervenes*, 1918. Text used by permission of Review and Herald® Publishing Association, Hagerstown, Maryland 21740.

SECTION FIVE: WE SHALL CALL UPON HIM, AND HE WILL ANSWER

"The Nine-Hour Prayer," by May Sheridan Gold from *Guideposts*, March 1977. Reprinted with permission from *Guideposts* magazine. Copyright © 1977 by Guideposts, Carmel, New York 10512.

"The Shetland Pony," by V. F. Smith. Published in *It Must Have Been an Angel*, by Marjorie Lewis Lloyd, 1978. Reprinted by permission of Pacific Press Publishing Association, Nampa, Idaho 83687. If anyone can provide knowledge of the whereabouts of V. F. Smith or surviving members of that family, please relay information to Joe Wheeler, care of WaterBrook Press.

"He Shall Keep Thee," by Lucille Taylor. Published in *The Youth's Instructor*, July 20, 1937. Reprinted by permission of Review and Herald® Publishing Association, Hagerstown, Maryland 21740. If anyone can provide knowledge of surviving Taylor family, please relay information to Joe Wheeler, care of WaterBrook Press.

"Prayer in Shorthand," by Minnie Waite Brown from *Guideposts,* February 1952. Reprinted with permission from *Guideposts* magazine. Copyright © 1952 by Guideposts, Carmel, New York 10512.

"The Yellow Kite," by Beverly Newman from *Guideposts,* August 1975. Reprinted with permission from *Guideposts* magazine. Copyright © 1975 by Guideposts, Carmel, New York 10512.

"Lost," by Grace Waters. Published in *The Youth's Instructor*, January 30, 1945. Reprinted by permission of Review and Herald® Publishing Association, Hagerstown, Maryland 21740. If anyone can provide knowledge of the whereabouts of surviving Waters family, please relay information to Joe Wheeler, care of WaterBrook Press.

"Please, God, Save Our Amy!" by Lois Olson from *Guideposts,* April 1977. Reprinted with permission from *Guideposts* magazine. Copyright © 1977 by Guideposts, Carmel, New York 10512.

"The Hand on My Shoulder," by Jerry Bond from *Guideposts,* May 1978. Reprinted with permission from *Guideposts* magazine. Copyright © 1978 by Guideposts, Carmel, New York 10512.

EPILOGUE

"God Put You on This Train!" by Joseph Leininger Wheeler. Copyright © 1998. Printed by permission of the author.